CURRICULUM AND SCHOOL TEACHER

CURRICULUM
AND
SCHOOL TEACHER

By

Dr. Marlow Ediger
Emeritus Professor of Education
Truman State University
201 West 22nd Street
North Newton KS 67117
United States of America
&
Dr. Digumarti Bhaskara Rao
M.Sc., M.A., M.A., M.Ed., Ph.D.
Principal & Professor
R.V.R. College of Education
D-43 (277) S.V.N. Colony
Guntur - 522 006 (India)
&
Member of Board of Studies in Education
Acharya Nagarjuna University
Nagarjuna Nagar - 522 510 (India)

DISCOVERY PUBLISHING HOUSE PVT. LTD.
NEW DELHI-110 002

Published by:
Tilak Wasan
DISCOVERY PUBLISHING HOUSE PVT. LTD.
4383/4B, Ansari Road, Darya Ganj
New Delhi-110 002 (India)
Phone : +91-11-23279245, 43596064-65
Fax : +91-11-23253475
E-mail : discoverypublishinghouse@gmail.com
namitwasan9@gmail.com
sales@discoverypublishinggroup.com
web : www.discoverypublishinggroup.com

First Edition: **2013**

Reprinted: **2018**

ISBN: 978-93-5056-247-5

Curriculum and School Teacher

Printed at:
Infinity Imaging Systems
Delhi

Dedicated
to

PROF. K. VIYANNA RAO
Vice-Chancellor
(in-charge)
Acharya Nagarjuna University
Krishna University

Preface

The school curriculum, now-a-days, has many different conceptions. It may include any educational experience and may also be conceived as a conversation, relationships and it is this phenomenon of plurality that is inherent in the new paradigm view of curriculum. It must be understood as encompassing not only those experiences that take place within schools, but the entire scope of formative experience both within and outside of schools. Further, it includes experiences that are not planned or directed, as well as experiences that are intentionally directed for the purposeful formation of right citizenry of society.

Many aspects of the aspects concerned to curriculum, school and teacher are discussed in this book. This book will be of great use to curriculum designers and teachers and administrators at school level.

Digumarti Bhaskara Rao

Contents

School Curriculum

There are a plethora of issues in the curriculum which need synthesizing. Relevant objectives developed for pupil attainment is a major problem. There are multiple facets here which need identification and attempted resolving.

Budget Cutting for Education

When recessions are in evidence, then considerable budget cutting is done on the state and federal levels of government to take care of shortfalls in revenue to balance budgets. Domestic spending too often gets the axe which hinders the less fortunate in society such as in education, Social Security, Medicare, and Medicaid, among other social programmes. The cries go out, "We cannot raise taxes." Taxes were not raised to fight two wars as in Iraq and Afghanistan and yet these are indeed expensive to support. With military spending being off the table for tax cuts, the clamour is to fine tune spending on domestic items. Cutting of taxes shows "fiscal responsibility". Even very small items may be cut such as spending money to support the arts. Once spending has been cut, it is very difficult to make up the deficiencies when times are more prosperous and increased revenue comes into the treasury. Taxes have been reduced much for big business and corporations, even preceding the recession. The outcomes need assessment and revaluation as to which budget items to keep and which to eliminate or reduce. The following problematic situations need attention and resolving;

- how much money should be allotted to social programmes including those which stress supporting the less fortunate in society?
- are fears maximized of enemy nations and of terrorists, thus making for continuing larger defense budgets?
- how much needs to be spent on infrastructure items such as fire and police protection, roads and bridges, as well as the general welfare?
- how much should be budgeted for natural disasters, at home and abroad, such as future tornados, hurricanes, earthquakes, sunamis, among others?
- which reforms are necessary in taxing income and wealth? With progressive taxation, the per cent paid would go up as income spikes. With regressive taxation, the lower income levels pay a much higher per cent of their money in taxes.

Paying for the costs of educating all pupils is expensive and yet these individuals will include leaders of the future. For a nation to succeed, a quality education is needed for all in order that the infrastructural needs are met. This includes scholarships and inexpensive loans for college/university students. Talents and abilities must not go to waste but used for the betterment of society. Public libraries, museums, as well as other sources of educational opportunities, should be well funded as these are sources of inservice education for adults as well as children (See Applegate and Applegate, 2011).

Technology in the Curriculum

Technology is greatly increasing in use in the school curriculum. Lap top computers for all pupils on selected grade levels, white boards, power point use, among others are the rule rather than the exception. There are justifiable reasons given for the wide use of multi-media which include the following:

- it assists pupils to keep abreast of innovations in the curriculum and in society. Low income children use technology in school as frequently as others. They may lack the many uses of technology in the home setting, thus making for gaps in opportunities among income levels of homes.

Multi-media provides pupils with opportunities to achieve more optimally. Teaching aids are necessary to assist pupils to attain objectives more readily. Technology use, too, might well be a learning style for pupils as compared to other methodologies. Technology utilization needs to be integrated into each unit of study and in as many lesson plans as feasible to optimize learner progress (See Dawson and Rakes, 2003).

Teachers need to be very knowledgeable in the use of multi-media, and pupils need guidance in operating and using technology. Inservice education is necessary in order that teachers possess the needed dispositions and skills to be advocates in implementing an updated curriculum. Any learning activity should not be emphasized for the sake of doing so, but rather to provide interesting and purposeful experiences which have relevance in the lives of pupils.

Higher Levels of Cognition and the Learner Pupils need to be actively involved in experiencing more complex levels of thinking. Mandated objectives deemphasize this, one reason being that that multiple choice test items are used to ascertain if pupils have achieved the stated ends of instruction. Multiple choice test items desire exact answers. In contrast, analytic thinking emphasizes breaking down a concept into component parts which may or may not contain precise information. "Fish" as a concept in a unit on Animals of the Sea, might well be separated into specifics such as gills, scales, bladder, fins, and back bone. Each specific may be discussed within a small group, followed by questions which become problems to solve such as, "Why are gills used in place of lungs to secure oxygen?" Research and brain storming might well result with the teacher recording each hypothesis. Pupils do become excited when engaged in problem solving if the topic generates interest and learners feel free to participate actively. When participating in problem solving, learners synthesize hypotheses with the emphasis being on holistic thought.

Thus, The concept "fish" might be contrasted with "reptiles." In beginning a discussion, it is good, for example, to see and then discuss the concept of "Fish" in the classroom aquarium. Memorization of subject matter is unimportant. Rather, it must be understood, useable and further the ongoing zest for achievement.

Ultimate Goals in the Curriculum

There are major goals which become objectives of instruction. To achieve them, there must be enabling learning opportunities. Thus in comprehension being the objective of reading subject matter, there are enabling activities such as word recognition strategies, meanings attached to understanding content read, critical and creative reading, as well as problem solving. Additional enablers include

- metacognition. Thus, the pupil reflects upon what has been learned to gain salient as compared to subordinate ideas, as well as assess accuracy of content gained. Metacognition stresses the importance of noticing what is not understood with intent upon filling the voids. The 21st century requires individuals who are motivated as well as use higher levels of cognition to improve employment opportunities and to develop appropriate citizenship skills. This includes being involved to improve society and improving in quality human relations.

- inductively securing the broad ideas of what has been read or discussed in order to obtain structure or key ideas. These generalizations assist in being upheld with supporting ideas. Too frequently, pupils read isolated facts which might soon be forgotten and/or not recalled, as needed, to pursue meaning or holism in what is being read (Ediger, 2011).

Conclusion

To secure indepth learnings, pupils must go beyond literal comprehension. They need to analyze, synthesize, and evaluate, as well as reflect upon subject matter acquired. In school and in society, pupils need to achieve skills in higher levels of cognition. In the future work place, increasingly more optimal levels of attainment are necessary.

REFERENCES

Applegate, Anthony J., and Mary DeKonty Applegate (2011), *"A Study of Thoughtful Literacy and the Motivation to Read,"* The Reading Teacher, (64) 226-235.

Dawson, C., and G. C. Rakes (2003), *"Technology Training and the Integration of Technology in Schools,"* Journal of Research on Technology in Education, 36 (1).

Ediger, Marlow (2011), *"Learning Stations in the Social Studies,"* Education, 131 (3), 467-470.

Ediger, Marlow, and D. Bhaskara Rao (2007), *Teaching Social Studies.* New Delhi, India: Discovery Publishing House.

Green, Bonnie A. (2010), *"Understand Schema, Understand Differences,"* Journal of Instructional Psychology (37), 133-145.

Ethics and Morality in Curriculum

There are salient standards for living which must be stressed in the curriculum. They serve as criteria in terms of what is the good life for all. When looking back to classical writers as well as modern times, the standards for ethics and morality has remained somewhat consistent and need to be studied by all learners. Universal criteria assists the self to become less egocentric in relating to others in society. All humans have worth and need to be treated with respect and caring. Too frequently, people think of the self in terms of what is moral and good. Militarism and war endeavours favour this line of thinking. The "others" in society be it individuals or nations must be brought to defeat so as to preserve one's personal freedoms regardless of death, destruction, and ruin that follows to the victims (Ediger and Rao, 2004).

Ethics and Morality in the Societal Realm

Socrates (470-399 BC) used a questioning procedure to assist individuals to ascertain moral truths, in ancient Athens. Thus, an inductive approach was used by Socrates and this came to be called the Socratic Method. Through questions raised by Socrates, individuals realized the lack of clarity and consistency of adhered to ethical beliefs. The Socratic method is used in the curriculum presently. Discovery methods are then used in place of lecture to help pupils learn. In Socrates time, there were skeptics who frowned at any attempt at truth. Socrates sought stability in morality and ethical behaviour in a time of growing skepticism. Socrates' thinking may be compared with a contemporary, named Gorgias who taught that

- nothing whatsoever exists
- if something exists, it cannot be known
- if it could be understood, it could not be communicated.

The Sophists were leaders at that time with beliefs stressing that each individual has his/her own truths, with nothing emphasizing universal truth. Everything is relative and "man is the measure of all things."

Aristotle (384–322 BC) advocated pure contemplation as the highest good for individuals to engage in. Contemplation involves thinking about ethics and morality. Pure contemplation emphasizes that one moves away from concrete situations of human made things and the natural environment to concentrate on the abstract and what makes for a good society. The goal stressed by Aristotle prior to and of lesser value than pure contemplation was the Golden Mean. This goal emphasized the here and the now with avoiding extremes in life such as taking foolish chances, being foolhardy, versus refraining from acting and doing in performing relevant deeds in society. There is a Golden Mean between the opposite ends of this continuum. Thus Aristotle would stress the Golden Mean in society and the highest good—pure contemplation—when individuals contemplate ethics and morality. Generally, the elite and upper class would have the most time and knowledge for contemplation to take place (See Brameld, 1955).

Stoicism, founded by Zeno (334-262 BC), advocated the good life as consisting of controlling personal feelings. Feelings could be controlled but happenings to the self had to be accepted. Thus, stoicism stressed not showing feelings toward anything that happened regardless of positive or negative occurrences. Individuals need to accept who and what they are and not complain, nor give blame for happenings one does not like. Life is like a drama in that it is short and one arrives on the stage with the good (wealth, for example) and the bad (an ugly face). Even for those occurrences which are liked, the individual should show no feelings. Stoicism then was an answer to social and personal dilemmas.

John Locke (1632-1704) emphasized four standards for the education of the elite or upper class. The highest standard was the virtuous person who has the qualities of being a good individual. This person is known for honesty, thrift, and quality behaviour. These individuals have a good reputation and are looked upon in a favourable manner. Next in saliency came wisdom. The person with wisdom has foresight in making wise judgments. These individuals do not come into poverty nor do they do shameful deeds. Third is good breeding. John Locke was critical of those who exhibited sheepish bashfulness in that they were shy and did not express themselves well in social situations. They were timid and reserved when communicating with others. The outgoing person with much confidence is wanted. Fourth, Locke stressed knowledge. He admitted to being "bookish," but felt there were three other traits being more important such as virtue, wisdom, and breeding. In his curriculum then, John Locke stressed four characteristics of a well educated gentleman (See Sahakian, 1968).

Jeremy Bentham (1748-1832) advocated "the greatest good for the greatest number" in the realm of society. This meant that governments should strive to make laws which benefit the largest number of people in society. Also, in judicial reform, Bentham worked to make punishments fit the crime rather than arbitrary rules and laws being promulgated. Uniformity in laws was then advocated by Bentham. For his day, "the greatest good for the greatest number was noble indeed. This is different than advocating human rights for the elite only or largely. In a democracy, minority rights, too, should and must be upheld, something that Bentham minimized (See Wayper, 1954).

David Hume (1711-1776) was a skeptic and questioned many actions and assumptions. He stressed, for example, that one cannot know cause and effect. Thus; if a person sees/hears two things as connected, the certainty of this cannot be determined. Striking a piano key, for example, is followed by the same sound continuously, according to an observer. But, this is customarily assumed to be true in that A causes B. But, the perceiver cannot see cause and effect.

As an extreme skeptic, does this mean that anarchy should prevail in an area or nation? Hume said that even if laws, rules, regulations are arbitrary in different states, the citizen must abide by these courses of action to make for civility. However, what are conceived to be absolutes cannot be proven and are subjective. There have been a plethora of philosophers who have looked for absolutes which are always true. A leader in this area, was Rene Descartes (1596-1650) who sought that which was always true, and he finally came up with the well known, "I think, therefore I am." This belief was established by Descartes after doubting everything possible, even his own existence. Descartes still had to come up with the God concept who, he felt, could not and would not deceive. God made it possible to accept that he (Descartes) was real since being one who thinks and a thinking human is real. No deception was involved here. The quest for universal certainty has alluded many individuals (See Ulich, 1950).

Immanuel Kant (1724-1804) believed in the Categorical Imperative which stated that whatever is wanted by the self should become a universal desire. Thus, if I want A, then A should be the goal for all people. If B is not wanted, then B should not be heaped upon others. Rudeness is not wanted for the self; then rudeness must not be passed onto others. Politeness is desired and then it should be a universal in behaviour. The Categorical Imperative is not an elective, but an imperative in human behaviour. It is an "ought" and not cause/effect in terms of human actions. The Categorical Imperative seemingly became an absolute in the thinking of many (See Bowyer, 1970).

Francis Bacon (1561-1626) was an early philosopher who emphasized accuracy in communication. He stressed four idols which hindered in arriving at truth:

- idols of the cave. The cave pertained to subjectivity and limits of the mind to arrive at accurate conclusions. Ideas conveyed need critical evaluation to come up with truths. Personal experiences must be assessed in terms of the larger society and world. Being gullible in listening to the thinking of others may be minimized in training the mind to stress critical and creative thinking.
- idols of the tribe. Within one's own acquaintances, statements are made and passed on which lack credibility. Culture then emphasizes half truths or fiction. A goal of culture must be to correct deficiencies in expressed content.
- idols of the market place. When people interact with others in the business world, careless and limitations in use of language might well be in the offing. Due to slovenly communication as well as simplicity in wording, individuals arrive at inaccuracies and distorted ideas. Careful use of meaningful language assists individuals to understand others better. Misunderstandings accrue when a lack of accuracy is in the offing.
- idols of the theater. Here, language is used in novel and in interesting ways whereby the listener might use

these ideas in vague ways in communicating with others. Presentations from theaters, if followed, bring on careless communication (Stumpf, 1973).

Basing his thinking on the mathematics model, Bertrand Russell, early twentieth century philosopher, emphasized that misunderstandings might well be minimized if precision in language was emphasized. At one point in his life, Russell stated that each word used orally should refer to something concrete. Thus, an abstract word should correlate with an object or item. These were called atomic facts. When two or more atomic facts are put together, the result is a molecular proposition. Too frequently, vague expressions, although used even in standard English, are meaningless. The presenter needs to be certain that preciseness in communication is in the offing. There is a relationship here between the thinking of Francis Bacon and Bertrand Russell. Both viewed the possibilities of using accuracy in language to communicate.

John Dewey (1859-1952) stressed the importance of experimentalism as a philosophy. Dewey believed that the quest for certainty of ideas was useless. One cannot know absolutes, but modified thinking occurs when solving problems. To solve a problem, the involved person or persons develops a tentative hypothesis and obtains information from a variety of sources to secure answers. The obtained information is used to test the hypothesis. As a result, the hypothesis may need revision or is accepted as is. New problems might arise in the ongoing problematic situation requiring an hypothesis, followed by its testing. Problem solving may definitely be used in attempting to solve ethical and moral dilemmas. Dewey used problem solving in his laboratory school at the University of Chicago and believed this procedure to be practical for pupils in the school and community setting (Dewey, 1916).

Conclusion

There are a myriad of questions to discuss pertinent to each of the philosophers mentioned in this writing:

- How do you like Socratic questioning as compared to lecture in a classroom?
- What have you come up with in using Contemplation as a means of getting at ethics and morality? Is this possible to do so?
- Might one's feelings be omitted/minimized when unfortunate/fortunate things happen, according to Stoicism? Is it possible to do so?
- Can virtue (John Locke) be learned by any person? What about in situations where violence in a community rules?
- Do you favour the "greatest good for the greatest number philosophy of Jeremy Bentham? Why or why not?
- Is it possible to be as great a skeptic as was David Hume?
- How is Immanuel Kant's Categorical Imperative like the Golden Rule?
- What are selected "idols" that you have heard in society?
- How helpful is John Dewey's problem solving in arriving at good ethical and moral behaviour? Why do you think that way?

Students should do much reading on each philosophy. A peer approach may be used whereby committee members assist each other in word recognition and meaning making. The subject matter needs to make sense and be usable to reflect upon being ethical and moral in behaviour. Concrete examples need to be given such as the teacher modeling Socratic procedures of instruction as compared to lecturing. Philosophy should be challenging as well as interesting.

REFERENCES

Bowyer, Carleton (1970), *Philosophical Perspectives for Education.* Glenview, Illinois: Scott, Foresman and Company.

Brameld, Theodore (1955), *Philosophies of Education in Cultural Perspective*. New York: Holt, Rinehart and Winston.

Dewey, John (1916), *Democracy and Education*. New York: The Macmillan Company.

Ediger, Marlow, and D. Bhaskara Rao (2004), *Philosophy and Curriculum.* New Delhi, India: Discovery Publishing House.

Sahakian, William S. (1968), *History of Philosophy*. New York: Barnes and Noble Books.

Stumpf, Samuel Eli (1973), *Philosophy, History and Problems*. New York: McGraw-Hill Book Company.

Ulich, Robert (1950), *History of Educational Thought*. New York: American Book Company.

Wayper, C. L. (1954), *Political Thought*. New York: Philosophical Library, Inc.

Collaboration Versus Individual Endeavours in Curriculum

Which is the better approach in pupil learning— working together in collaborative situations or working by the self in ongoing learning activities? Howard Gardner (1993), Harvard University psychologist, emphasized that these are two different intelligences. Collaboration is preferred by selected pupils in learning. These learners do best when working in a small group to complete ongoing activities and experiences. Individuals working by the self may have this intelligence as a preference. Individually, pupil achievement is at a higher level as compared to working cooperatively with others.

Collaboration Versus Individual Endeavours

In working collectively within a lesson/unit of study, pupils experience a social situation. Quality interaction among participants is needed to agree upon objectives in an activity as well as making plans to achieve these objectives. Further interaction is necessary to carry out the plans to fruition as well as evaluation procedures must be developed to evaluate the final product as well as processes used along the way. Co-operatively developed standards are necessary in collaboration which include:

- all members need to contribute as much as possible;
- contributions need to circulate among members and not between two pupils only;
- politeness and acceptance of each other must prevail;
- an attitude of assisting each other to succeed is crucial;
- processes used in committee work need to be appraised regularly.

Progress reports should be made periodically to notice formative achievement as well as to aid in sequential attainment. Collaborative endeavours will succeed if appropriate standards are followed in ongoing activities. The role of the teacher is to observe pupils carefully in terms of desired goals as well as provide assistance as needed to help reamers to persevere in an orderly manner. The processes involved are as salient as the products produced from collaborative work. Pupils, too, are responsible for endorsing criteria for effective committee work. Both product and processes emphasize learning and stress goal attainment within an ongoing unit of study. Quality experiences assist achievement and progress. Thus, the topic or project must be interesting to pupils and involve active engagement. Pupils are not passive recipients but are engaged in the ongoing activity. Information being processed must relate to the pupil's own sphere of purpose in order that relevancy is in evidence. The purpose is related to the learner's interests and thus propels effort in achievement. The learner is not passive in receiving knowledge and skills, but rather is an active being who seeks and finds that which is relevant and purposeful.Then too, meaning theory becomes salient in that the learner attempts to find what makes sense. Attaining meaning as well as understanding what is taught is vital to the learner. If pupils engage in collaborative lessons/units of study or if individual efforts are put forth, the pupils must seek purpose and meaning within an interesting experience. Collaboration and individual endeavours should assist pupils to attain objectives in the curriculum and provide background experiences for ensuing learning activities.

With collaboration, the pupil is in an advantage of developing feelings of belonging. In Maslow's hierarchy (1954), the following needs are listed for human beings:

- physiological (nutrition, shelter, sleep and rest, thirst alleviation, and proper clothing)
- safety (freedom from danger and abuse)
- belonging (wanting to be an accepted member of a group)
- esteem (desire for recognition and reward for goal accomplishment)
- wishing to be the kind of person desired.

The desired need fulfilment may be in any order of the above asterisked items, but generally follow the order given and they are interrelated. Cooperative endeavours does emphasize the importance of achieving feelings of belonging. Thus, persons do not wish to be isolates but be an accepted member of a group. By working together on selected tasks, pupils develop increased proficiency in working with others, providing the learning environment is suitable. Thus, appropriate standards must be followed. The writer in supervising university student teachers observed where pupils in a committee were on task rather continuously. They were exited and enticed with the task being pursued. When recess time came, these participants wanted to keep working on the ongoing activity. Interest made for motivation as well as acceptable peers made for quality human relations. The writer also noticed whereby small group work did not materialize to achieve goals. The following were reasons for the failure in the collaborative endeavour:

- seemingly the student teacher and the cooperating teacher did not introduce the project appropriately to secure interests of learners.

- pupils did not understand their respective roles in small group work.
- there were pupils in the small group who did not respect each other; definite cases of rudeness were noticed readily. Membership in a collaborative endeavour need to learn to work together if goals are to be accomplished. It may be necessary to put pupils in a committee who function well together; later, pupils, as they progress, may be more accepting of others.
- those who are isolates, initially, might be placed with others who are highly accepting of others. The teacher and pupils in the committee must evaluate if all are participating adequately. If this does not occur, diagnosis must be emphasized to ascertain causes with remediation following.

There are a plethora of activities involving collaborative experiences. One committee made a model farm scene in a social studies unit. Learners expressed purpose in doing the model being inherent in the objectives of the project. They carefully planned the project before initiating the activity. Accepting the purpose or reasons for doing the model, pupils do progress in the experience. Evaluation was continuous as the work commenced with pupils raising questions about what did not possess clarity. Pupils do need to establish meaningful learning in sequential steps when engaged in the project method. In science, four pupils were working collaboratively in developing a model volcano, folds, and faults, in an ongoing unit of study titled, "Changes on the Earth's Surface" Much research went into developing the project such as securing information through and from internet use, textbooks/library books, journal articles, video tapes, and DVDs, among others. The completed projects were open to viewing by pupils in other classrooms. In a mathematics class, five pupils collaboratively developed models of a cone, pyramid, and a cylinder. By using a hands on approach in learning, pupils seemingly learned more about each space figure as compared to looking at and discussing textbook drawings and then finding the volume of each. Collaboration, too, stresses art work, human relations, eye hand co-ordination, as well as personal responsibility. Aygotsky (1933-1978) advocated collaborative work for pupils; in this way, ideas circulate and "bounce off the minds of participants." Learning, then, occurs within a social setting with pupils learning from each other as well as from the self. John Dewey (1916), also, advocated pupils learning in group settings. In his laboratory school at the University of Chicago, as early as 1896, pupils engaged in problem solving activities.

In comparing collaborative learning with individual endeavours, the latter also has responsibilities of careful listening and interacting to secure the most out of teacher explanations, task identification, understanding the objectives, assignment to achieve objectives, and appraisal procedures to optimize learning. The learner must ask for clarification of what is not understood in order to develop sequence in achieving. As a style of learning, the pupil has opportunities to pace his/her progress as individual differences provide. The kinds of activities can be the same such as engaging in the project method, problem solving, use of computers and technology, among others. The pupil does not need to wait on others to finish their segment of work as is true of collaborative endeavours. Also, these individuals do not need to:

- keep pace with others when it is difficult to do so
- feel inferior as compared to others who shine in the committee setting
- worry about criticism from peers.

When viewing the individual in society, it is quite obvious that a person interacts with others at the work place and with others in different clubs and organizations. Thus, it is very salient to be able to interact harmoniously with others in collaborative endeavours. Then too, each person needs to be able to find what to do individually. Thus hobbies, talents, as well as personal interests, may find oneself in finding what to do individually. Individuals work together with others as well as by the self. The classroom teacher then must assist pupils to do both well — work and interact well collaboratively as well as use spare and leisure time well. Then too, later at the work place the individual may need to work by the self (Ediger and Rao, 2007).

Conclusion

The teacher must provide a classroom which assists pupils well in social and individual endeavours. Classroom management then becomes important in doing the following:

- structuring the classroom with a variety of interesting learning activity which meet objectives. These materials provide learning activities for collaborative and individual work.
- discuss with clarity roles for each person to perform, be it individual or collaborative, leaving much room for creative and critical thinking as well as problem solving
- model behaviours which may not be understood by learners
- evaluate pupil pursuits when monitoring learner behaviour in achievement
- assist pupils as needed in order that quality sequence in learning is in evidence.

REFERENCES

Dewey, John (1916), *Democracy and Education*. New York: The Macmillan Company.

Ediger, Marlow, and D. Bhaskara Rao (2007), *Teaching Social Studies*. New Delhi, India: Discovery Publishing House.

Gardner, Howard (1993), *Multiple Intelligences: Theory into Practice*. New York: Basic Books.

Maslow, A.H. (1954), *Motivation and Personality*. New York: Harper and Row.

Vygotsky, Len (1933-1978), *Mind in Society* : The Development of Higher Psychological Processes. Cambridge, Massachusetts: Harvard University Press.

Philosophy and Curriculum Organization

There are several philosophies involved in organizing the curriculum. How the curriculum is organized may mean much to pupils in the school setting. Teachers, school administrators, and curriculum directors need to study, analyze, and implement that which assists learners to achieve as optimally as possible. In an era when public schools are asked to aid pupil progress in passing mandated tests as well as avoid dropouts from school, it behooves planners of the school curriculum to provide necessary inputs to assist all to be successful learners (Ediger,2010).

Plans of Curricular Organization

One of the oldest methods in organizing the curriculum was to use the separate subjects approach which is still popular presently. The philosophy here stressed the saliency of keeping each academic discipline separate with its objectives of instruction, learning opportunities for pupils to achieve these objectives, and evaluation procedures which measure pupil progress. A watered down curriculum results when each discipline loses its clarity and uniqueness. There are essential bodies of knowledge from these disciplines which each pupil needs to master, according to advocates. William Chandler Bagley (1874-1946) Emphasized the separate subjects curriculum and essentialism. He believed strongly that each academic discipline should maintain its integrity and not be integrated with others since this simplified knowledge and selected academic areas would then be minimized. The No Child Left Behind (NCLB) law of 2002 of USA mandated testing of reading and mathematics in grades three through eight for pupils to meet standards for promotion purposes. Science was added in 2009; this left social studies out as a member of the big four curriculum areas. Dr. Bagley was opposed to the social studies as a curriculum area due to its emphasis upon integrating content in relating subject matter areas. Rather, he wanted history to be taught as a separate subject. Dr. Bagley believed that only exacting content be taught such as in mathematics, history with its names, dates, places, and salient events, as well as the different branches of science. Thus, social studies stressed vague content in its implementation. Dr. Bagley was opposed to:

- lax discipline in the classroom
- the correlated and fused curriculum, to be discussed later
- the interests of students being heavily emphasized. Bagley wanted stability.
- an activity centered curriculum which John Dewey stressed.
- student input in planning objectives, learning activities, and evaluation procedures (Wahlquist, 1942).

But, essentialism lives on under different names such as in mandated academic areas. Thus, a body of knowledge and skills has been identified which all school pupils should master and be tested upon. The measurability of mandated testing comes from the measurement movement advocated by E. L. Thorndike (1874-1946) and B.F. Skinner

(1902-1986). The essentials or basics in mandated objectives stress the importance of

- precise objectives to be used by teachers in emphasizing targets to aim for when teaching.
- aligning instruction with these highly specific objectives.
- testing to see how well students have achieved.
- the test results are stated numerically in terms of percentiles, as well as grade/age equivalent scores, when compared with the norm group listed in the Manual.
- grade and district as well as state averages may be compared (in the media) with other schools by grade levels, school districts, and states, in the Nation's Report Card.
- teacher achievement, compared with other classrooms, may be evaluated based on his/her classroom test scores (Ediger, 2008).

The separate subjects curriculum may be emphasized with/without measurement philosophy of education and the following summary statements may be made:

- students may become highly familiar with an academic discipline.
- students may develop a deeper understanding of that academic discipline being studied.
- students may achieve sequence in one academic discipline without interference from other subject matter areas.
- students may understand the scope of a single academic discipline better by limiting content to one subject matter area.
- students may focus upon using the methods of acquiring subject matter as advocated by academicians, such as historians, scientists, mathematicians, among others (Ediger and Rao, 2003).

A second plan in organizing the curriculum emphasizes relating two academic disciplines in teaching (Ragan and Shepherd, 1982). A block of time may stress fusion or students perceiving the relatedness of two academic areas. A ninety minute block may then be devoted to teaching history and literature. This doubles the amount of time in this block as compared with the usual forty five minute period traditionally. The history and literature teacher, for example, might then co-operatively plan the objectives and subject matter to be taught. The Great Depression and the literature written during that time may be fused, and not taught separately. This might well be a good way to have proper perspective in relating literature to the time it was written. How much relationship of knowledge should pupils perceive? No doubt, it is a role of educational philosophy to determine the degree of integration of subject matter. Why should there be fusion and other interrelated subject matter be taught?

- pupils perceive the whole of knowledge, not separate categories
- pupils find it easier to remember content if they can relate it to other academic disciplines
- pupils become increasingly creative when engaging in combining academic disciplines
- pupils find knowledge more useful when fusion/ integration of subject matter occurs in learning by discovery.

The following summary statements indicate the advantages of using a block of time in teaching:

- teachers would teach fewer subjects and teach them in greater depth.
- teachers would be responsible for fewer students, such as eighty as compared to 175 in the separate subjects curriculum. Diplomas would be awarded upon mastery of subject matter.

- teachers need to know each student well and realize there are individual differences
- teachers must realize students possess different learning styles.
- teachers need to provide situations with many questions for students to ponder upon (Watkins,1990).

A third philosophical plan of curricular organization emphasizes the unified curriculum whereby teachers, school administrators, and students, believe in subject matter increasingly losing its boundaries and borders. Knowledge is perceived holistically by learners, not fragmented. Thus, history, geography, science, literature, and mathematics become unified. A team of teachers might then plan the objectives, learning activities, and evaluation procedures for any given unit of study. For example, if students are studying a unit on The Age of Discovery (history), place location in geography may be brought in, in terms of where these discoveries took place. Science discoveries, such as Galileo's experiments in the 1600s on gravity from the leaning tower of Pisa, bring on much student interest and a myriad of experiments may be brought in to the ongoing unit of study. With science experiments, mathematics is the language of expression in terms of measurement of phenomenon. Developmentally appropriate literature may be brought in such as *The Prince* by Machiavelli. The degree of unification of subject matter emphasizes a philosophy of education. How do students learn best in curriculum organization? Is it with the separate subjects, the fused or unified curriculum? (See Ediger, 2006).

There is one additional plan which needs discussion pertaining to curriculum organization and that is problem solving. Problem solving stress the identification and solving of lifelike problems. John Dewey (1859-1953) was a leading proponent of problem solving with experimentalism as a philosophy of education. Dr. Dewey had a laboratory school at the University of Chicago in the late 1890s which stressed experimentalism. This philosophical school of thought emphasized the following:

- change is paramount in school and in society
- school and society are integrated, not separate entities
- schools need to stress the practical since individuals live in the societal arena
- pupils in school are actively involved in learning, not passive recipients of knowledge
- life consists of solving personal and social problems
- ultimate reality cannot be known but experiences are knowable (Dewey, 1916).

In the school setting, students identify problems, develop related hypotheses, and these are tried out, not through test taking, but in lifelike situations. The following school situations involve problem solving:

- developing standards of conduct for students interacting with each other
- planning and doing a project directly related to an ongoing unit of study
- organizing and implementing a formal or informal dramatization
- constructing a model pertaining to a concept or generalization being studied
- working co-operatively in pursuing an ongoing activity.

Problems arise within an ongoing experience which require clarification, an hypothesis, and an approach in its evaluation. Experimentalists are also strong in looking at the consequences of an act or action.

Conclusion

Teachers and supervisors need to study and plan effective methods of organizing the curriculum. Criteria which need emphasizing in organizing the curriculum include the following:

- does it minimize one or more academic areas?
- will it assist pupils to establish meaning in an ongoing activity?
- will learners become more motivated and perceive purpose in learning?

The plan chosen may be used for one academic area for a single unit or part of a unit of study. Other approaches may be added as needed. Flexibility in organization of the curriculum makes it possible to adapt each to assist optimal learner achievement and progress.

REFERENCES

Dewey, John (1916), *Democracy and Education.* New York: The MacMillan Company.

Ediger, Marlow (2010), *"Issues in Social Studies,"* International Journal of Educational Research, Development and Extension, 1 (1), 43-49.

Ediger, Marlow (2008), *"Psychology of Parental Involvement in Reading,"* Journal of Instructional Psychology, Reading Improvement, 45 (1), 46-52.

Ediger, Marlow, and D. Bhaskara Rao (2003), *Philosophy and Curriculum.* New Delhi, India: Discovery Publishing House.

Ediger, Marlow (2006), *"Teaching Mathematics in the High School Setting,"* College Student Journal, 39 (4), 711-715.

Ragan, William, and Gene Shepherd (1982), *Modern Elementary Curriculum.* New York: Holt Rinehart and Winston.

Wahlquist, John T. (1942), *The Philosophy of American Education.* New York: Ronald Publishing Company.

Watkins, Beverley T. (1990), *"An Education Professor Tries to Put on His Fantasy School into Effect,"* The Chronicles of Higher Education, November 7, p. A3.

Philosophical Implications in Choosing Learning Activities

There salient implications for philosophy in selecting learning activities for pupils. Each activity is based upon a selected school of thought in the philosophy of education. Then too, philosophies might well overlap; some may not be as clearly defined as others. Teachers, supervisors, and school administrators must study, evaluate, and then appraise different schools of thought. Being highly knowledgeable assists the decision-making process in providing for individual differences among learners be it in interests, talents, and intelligences. Learning styles, too, differ when emphasizing one style of learning as compared to others.

Learning Opportunities in the Curriculum

Perhaps, the oldest type of activity is for the younger children to observe adults in hunting and gathering societies. Direct observation was involved in securing adequate wild life and plants for food. The adult helped the young to become increasingly proficient in obtaining enough food. Knowledge and skill was stressed here, and success in endeavours was salient to prevent hunger/starvation.

In present day schools many educators stress selected direct experiences for pupils. Pupils, for example, with teacher guidance are engaged in gardening experiences. Even elementary age pupils are learning techniques of being gardeners. In a recent issue of the Hutchinson, Kansas News (July, 15, 2010), intermediate grade pupils with teacher guidance in selected local schools were growing radishes and peppers, in co-operation with Kansas State University School of Agriculture, on an experimental basis. Newton, Kansas Public Schools supervises their Rural Life School at nearby Walton, in which meals are served using the school's homegrown fruits and vegetables.

There are diverse beliefs in selecting activities for pupils to attain objectives of instruction. E. L. Thorndike (1874-1949) was instrumental in advocating precisely stated objectives. The specificity of these objectives made it so the teacher could determine if pupils had/had not achieve an objective after instruction. Thus, Thorndike receives much credit for starting the measurement movement in education, "Whatever exists, exists in some amount, and if it exists in some amount, it can be measured." With the measurement movement, many tests were developed to measure pupil achievement in different academic areas. The present day accountability movement has built upon measuring learner achievement with teachers being held accountable for pupils doing well on mandated tests. In emphasizing measurement philosophy of education, objectives must be stated with clarity so no doubt exists in terms of their meaning. Teachers then know what exact target to aim toward in teaching pupils. With mandated objectives, the teacher chooses the learning activities, but not the objectives of instruction. Nor does the teacher ascertain tests to be used in measuring teacher success. The tests as well as the objectives are written on the state/ national levels (Ediger and Rao, 2003).

With teacher designed classroom objectives and tests, he/ she has more control over the curriculum. The learning activities, too, are teacher chosen. The measurement movement tended to advocate using:

- standardized tests to measure achievement. There is uniformity here in test items, directions given for test taking, time limits in taking the test, the same scoring key for multiple choice test items, for pupils in any age level.
- aligning learning activities with the objectives. This stressed the importance in not straying from the objectives of instruction.
- testing to determine if the objectives have been achieved. Test results may be compared state by state and/or compare school districts within a state when published in the news media. This may be labeled as the nation's score card.

There are plethora of weaknesses in the mandated testing approach of instruction. It places much faith in choosing the right objectives by those specialists removed from the local school, prior to instruction. There is little leeway for input from teachers in terms of *what* to teach or for pupils to identify problems to solve. What is tested is what will be taught has become a slogan. This omits content from academic disciplines not being a part of the test. Then too, it omits qualities which are difficult to test such as good attitudes, caring for others, and being considerate. When making comparisons among teachers based on their pupils test results, there are differences in the makeup of learners within a classroom. Pupils tend to receive lower test results if they come from low income homes and/or come from minority groups. These pupils have not had the opportunities to learn which learners have had from favourable income levels. Money buys reading materials for the home, travelling to see distant places from home base, lessons for extra curricular learnings such as instrumental and dance, among others (See Stiggins, 1997).

Somewhat toward the other end of the continuum from the measurement moment is constructivism. Constructivists have much less confidence in testing to notice achievement. They believe that pupils create their own knowledge and skills. As the learning activity continues within an ongoing unit of study, the pupil sequences learnings and reveals questions which need answers. The answers are not provided by the teacher, rather he/ she assists pupils to locate what is needed such as in a reference source, or the teacher may ask a question in return whereby the pupil may learn the necessary content inductively. The teacher must be well versed in subject matter and reference sources to use constructivism as a philosophy of instruction. The questions need to be sequential to assist pupils to achieve inductively. Learning by discovery is a key component of constructivism. The teacher not only enables, but also encourages pupil achievement (Ediger, 2010).

With constructivism, the teacher does not lecture, unless it amounts to a brief explanation in helping learners move forward. Criticism and rudeness interfere with learning and the classroom environment must be very supportive and encouraging. The teacher's role is not to be "a sage on the stage," but rather one who facilitates and motivates learner progress. Teacher observation is utilized to appraise pupil achievement by noticing progress and assisting when needed. This leaves ample room for problem solving and projects where pupils individually and collectively order their very own sequences. Modeling by the teacher may be necessary at different points in using either method.

Problem Solving and The Project Method

Problem solving approaches was advocated by John Dewey (1859-1953), late professor of education at Columbia University. Dr. Dewey believed that school and society not be separated from each other, and problem solving emphasized life itself. Individuals/groups are always identifying and solving problems where change is paramount. Certainly, this is true in:

- selecting a vocation/job or position.
- attending higher education or entering the work place.
- choosing a marriage partner.
- buying/renting a house or an automobile.
- securing finances to purchase needed housing and transportation.
- purchasing groceries and living within one's budget.

There are problems then which take considerable time in solving whereas others may be solved rather quickly. Dr. Dewey in his laboratory school at the University of Chicago stressed problem solving with flexible steps involved here such as clearly selecting a problem so that capability exists in its possible solving. Vague, hazy problems do not lend themselves to further action. Once the problem possesses clarity, then an hypothesis is developed. The hypotheses is tentative and subject to modification. Data is gathered from a variety of reference sources, be they concrete, semi-concrete, or abstract. The information gathered must be in answer to the problem and might well lead to refuting, modifying, or accepting the original hypothesis. The accepted hypothesis must be tried out in a real live situation. New problems might well arise along the way. Problem solving emphasizes pupils with teacher guidance selecting the problem as well as the teacher being a helper in guiding problem solving experiences. Dr. Dewey stressed experimentalism as a philosophy of education. Thus, the following principles are followed in the instructional arena:

- the pupil is an active learner, not a passive recipient of knowledge.
- problem solving is a lifelong endeavour
- absolute knowledge is not possible, but tentative solutions are. They are continually tested in action and lead to more certainty.
- the consequences of any action need to be evaluated before progressing to a new endeavour (Dewey, 1916).

Dewey lived in an era of rapid change. He was born in 1859 with automobiles arriving on the scene in the early 1900s. During the 1930s, cars already came out with electric lights, starters, hydraulic brakes, and heaters. This made for rapid changes in society such as travelling for recreation purposes, more restaurants and hotels, and car agencies selling automobiles. Farming changed rapidly from using draft horses in pulling implements to tractors on steel wheels to those with rubber tires, lights, starters. Combines increasingly were in number to harvest grain in a single operation, replacing grain binders which cut grain and made bundles which were hauled to a stationary threshing machine. Here, the grain was separated from the straw and chaff as well as being augured into a trailer and then shoveted by hand into a grain bin. During the 1940s, grain augurs powered by gasoline engines augured the grain from the truck into a grain bin with no shoveling by hand involved. By the time, Dewey died in 1953, society was heavily mechanized and doing much of the work with the use of machines.

A project method was developed by William Heard Kilpatrick (1871-1964), late professor at Columbia University. He used as a model that students in agriculture classes had projects such as swine, cattle, sheep, among others, and applied these examples to the public schools. Thus, in an ongoing unit in the school setting, pupils with teacher guidance identified projects to be developed. The project might stress making a solar collector in science. Generally, pupils worked collectively since social development of pupils was held in high esteem. They needed to follow up in developing a plan in making the model. Pupils needed to perceive purpose in the planning and doing the model. The teacher served as a guide and facilitator and it was up to learners to engage wholeheartedly in this endeavour. Involved pupils then carried through with the carefully designed plan. Pupils then sequenced their very own learnings under teacher supervision. Criteria were devised to evaluate the model.

The project method stressed the importance of:

- securing pupil interests in making the model
- utilizing a variety of learning activities in doing the model such as reading, writing, listening, and oral communication.
- pupils working harmoniously with quality interaction on the project.
- learners being meticulous in planning and doing.
- responsibility on the learner's part.
- pupils being co-operative when working with others.
- a child/pupil centered curriculum (See Bowyer, 1970).

Dr. Kilpatrick's method may be contrasted with textbook usage in that the teacher selects and implements content deemed to be important in teaching from the basal. The teacher is solely in control of the class and may fear relinquishing this method for fear of pupils misbehaving. The interest of pupils is felt to be relatively unimportant and purpose for learning resides within the teacher, not pupils. Sequence, too, also resides in the thinking of the teacher; a teacher centered curriculum is in the offing with the textbook determining what is to be taught.

During the early 20th century with much debate on educational philosophy, there were educators who emphasized a strict subject centered approach in teaching such as William Chandler Bagley (1874-1946). Bagley believed there were basics or essentials for all pupils to acquire. Each academic discipline should be taught as a separate subject, not fused or integrated with other disciplines. Correlating different academic disciplines weakened inherent subject matter to be taught in the public school setting Bagley opposed lax discipline in schools and this was stressed in his opposing the interest factor in learning. Discipline should emphasizing learning content and not catering to the child's whims. In society, work needs to be completed if the interests are there or not. Bagley believed in a stable curriculum, not one of continual change. Activity centered curricula such as those advocated by Dewey and Kilpatrick should be replaced with solid academic learnings. A properly certified, competent teacher should select objectives, learning opportunities, and evaluation procedures. This procedure was opposite than teacher/pupil planning of the curriculum Instructional decisions involve the responsibility of the teacher, not pupils, according to Bagley.

Essentialists like Bagley believed strongly in passing on the basics to future generations. There were educators involved in identifying the basics in literature, history, geography, science, and mathematics. The present day trend of mandated objectives certainly emphasizes that there is a body of knowledge and skills which all pupils should master (See Thayer, 1970).

There are also educators who recommend an activity centered approach in teaching, somewhat related to Dewey and Kilpatrick. A learning centers procedure emphasizes decision-making by pupils in an ongoing unit of study. Thus, a classroom may provide four centers with suggested tasks listed for each. For example, four to five tasks may be listed on a card at each center, and after the learning centers have been introduced, pupils may choose the center and task to work on, be it individual or committee endeavours. There are more tasks than what any pupil can complete so that choices truly exist. The teacher is a supervisor and helps pupils to be on task. If a pupil fails to do so, the teacher assists the learner to pursue and accomplish. Pupils sequence their own achievement and teacher observation is used to assess progress. Pupils here are active learners and seek out their very own interests in sequential task selection.

At the different learning centers, there are attempts at providing for individual differences with the following kinds of activities available for pupil choice:

- hands on experiences as well as learning academic content
- art activities directly related to the unit being emphasized
- oral and written work
- reading experiences such as library book and internet content
- listening experiences such as following directions in constructing a model (See Joyce, *et. al.,* 1983).

The Standards Movement in Education

The No Child Left Behind (NCLB) federal mandate of 2002 emphasized each state develop standards or objectives for all pupils to achieve within their respective borders. Aligned tests measured achievement in grades three through eight in reading, arithmetic, and science, as well as an exit test in high school. Pupils needed to pass the tests to be promoted to the next higher grade level. The exit test on the secondary level must be passed to receive a high school diploma. The standards were the same for all pupils on a specific grade level as well as the standards for measurement. Thus, for testing, the directions were the same, the time limits for test taking, as well as the key for scoring the results were also the same. Test results for special education results as well as for English Language Learners (ELL) were disagreegated to notice if adequate progress had been made here. Schools were also required to meet Adequate Yearly Progress (AYP) by the year 2014. Measurement Theory was certainly in evidence here in that learner and school performance can be measured, using standardized tests (Ediger, 2006).

The Common Core Standards, no doubt, will replace NCLB in time. Common Core Standards stress the same standards for all states within each grade level. The complaints with NCLB standards were the following:

- it was anarchic in that each state determined standards regardless of what other states were doing.

- there were great differences among the states in terms of what was required and measured.
- differences existed in terms of percentage of pupils passing tests for promotion.
- states differed in percentage meeting adequate yearly progress (See Ray, 2006).

With Common Core Standards, there will be disadvantages with regions differing on what is salient to be taught. The standards may be uniform nationwide, but pupils differ from each other in achievement. Should all pupils attain the same standards when learners may differ much from each other in interests, aptitudes, and abilities? Can the teacher make up for these differences with stimulating (learning activities? Is it possible to develop high quality standards nationwide? These are questions which good answers from advocates of common core standards.

To achieve common core standards, the teacher needs to select learning opportunities which engage and are of interest to pupils. Diverse levels of achievement need to be provided for in the classroom. Thus, the chosen activities need to harmonize with the learning styles of pupils. They also need to be perceived as

- being relevant and purposeful
- meaningful and on the developmental level of the pupil
- being aligned with the standards as well as leave room for pupil's questions.

There are issues in the testing movement which certainly do need resolving. Which curriculum areas should be tested? NCLB was narrow in scope here, in that reading and mathematics were requirements initially; this was broadened to include science. Social studies was omitted as were physical education, music, and art. Also, there was criticism of moral/ ethical dimensions being ignored such as good citizenship and the caring person. Methods of teaching, too frequently, emphasized studying for NCLB tests through rote learning and memorization.

Each school of thought may be appraised in terms of the traditional four philosophical classifictions. The curriculum will be discussed in analyzing through the lens of realism, idealism, experimentalism, and existentialism.

Realism traditionally has stressed that human beings can know reality as it truly is. Thus, a pupil secures a replica of the natural and social environment Realism has science as its basis and rests upon the concepts of precision and exactness. Numerals are generally used to describe observations as is true of test scores—percentiles, grade age equivalents, stanines, standard deviations, and percentages. The world of science such as chemistry stresses precision in describing the number of electrons, protons, neutrons, elements, and compounds within different kinds of matter.

For the classroom teacher, the objectives of instruction must possess clarity and stated in measurable terms. Learning activities are aligned with the stated objectives. Progress is measured if a pupil has/has not secured the correct answer, generally in a multiple choice or word problem solving format. Either the learner was/was not correct in responding. A pupil's score may be compared with others in the classroom. The achievement of one classroom may be compared with others. School districts and states might well be compared also to perceive progress. Teachers may be evaluated on pupil success in test results, such as in merit pay proposals.

With realism, teachers teach toward ends (objectives) and pupil test scores reveal the degree of success of the classroom teacher (See, National Research Council, 1995).

Idealism, a second philosophy emphasizes an idea/ideal centered curriculum for pupils and has the social sciences as a foundation. The ideas are broader than those of the precision based realism. Literature and history, in particular, may be used as illustrations. Morality and universal ethics might well be discussed in viewing pros and cons of actions taken by nations, states, regions, as well as of individuals. For example, Immanuel Kant in the eighteenth century, emphasized the Categorical Emperative, which stressed a universal standard. Here, the individual should want as an ethical/moral principle for all as he/she desires for the self The Golden Rule rule, "Do unto others as you would want them to do to you." This indicates that idealism is not only idea, but also ideal centered. Ideals in life form the basis in interacting with others. History and literature tend themselves well to analyzing actions in terms of the Categorical Imperative.

Each academic discipline may be discussed in terms of being idea centered. Pythagoras an ancient Athens philosopher emphasized ultimate reality as being a number for each entity. Thus, in geometry a point may be represented by the abstract "one." Two points represented a line whereas three points indicated a triangle and four points a square. Mathematical ideas may be discussed in the abstract completely in an idealist's thinking. Plato (424-344 BC) was a true idealist. He emphasized the sensible world of objects that human beings see every day like a chair, table, a door, among many other things in one's surroundings, inferior to the Forms. The Forms existed above the world of sense and was represented by perfection. Thus the things in the here and the now are an imperfect representation of the perfect, chair, table, door, and so on. The Forms represented the ideal and not the temporary sensible things on this planet earth. Plato's idealism is further stressed when he divided workers in the economic world into three categories. Each person then was born/educated into one of three categories—leaders in *government* who ruled his ideal republic. These individuals had the most talent and ability for their role in society. On a lower level were the *guardians* of the state whose duty it was to defend the republic against all enemies. The third and lowest fevel were the *workers* who provided goods and services for all members in the republic. These three categories made for balance in the republic whereby talents were used which were possessed. In present day thinking of idealists, the following major generalizations in curriculum development might well be emphasized:

- mental development of pupils come first with diverse academic disciplines providing challenging content to pupils.
- pupils might then become increasingly motivated to reach ideals in learning.
- an academically inclined teacher needs to select and teach subject matter which involves pupils. Indepth knowledge and skills must be taught.
- the teacher is a model for pupils to emulate in the subject centered curriculum.
- thought provoking subject matter needs to be taught with the ideals of the good, the true, and the beautiful as broad goals.
- character development should assist pupils to move in the direction of the ideal or the absolute. Individuals are perceived to be finite and moving toward the infinite. A process is involved here.
- the learner must be perceived holistically intellectually, socially, emotionally, and physically, as well as morally/ ethically (See Ozman and Cramer, 1990).

Existentialism, a third philosophy, emphasizes the individual first of all exists or is, and then attempts to find his/her purposes in life. These are not given, but must be sought in time. There are no absolutes in life and truth resides within the learner. Constructivists emphasize the saliency of the individual developing truths as he/she progresses in education. The teacher is a guide and stimulates pupils to achieve, but does not lecture as "a sage on the stage". Rather, the teacher assists pupils to raise questions pertaining to what is not understood, and then assists learners to find necessary information. Thus, knowledge is subjective, rather than objective as the realist contends. The teacher helps pupils to find freedom in learning. Morality and ethics are key components in the curriculum and each pupil needs to take a position on relevant purposes in life. To let others make the choices robs the individual of being human. He/she must do the choosing. The learner chooses his/her own destiny in an open ended world. The inner directed person makes choices and decisions; however, these choices are made on the basis of much thought and background information. The inner directed person looks at the consequences of choices/decisions made. How do these affect others? They may make for personal unhappiness, joy, or contentment but one cannot escape from choosing; life demands that one chooses, from among alternatives. Morality and ethics are salient in decision-making, not personal self gratification. No other person is responsible for what transpires as a result of making decisions, but the one making the choice.

The curriculum must be quite open ended according to existentialists. Pupils need to be heavily involved in choosing objectives, learning opportunities, and appraisal procedures with learners choosing their destiny. The existentialist curriculum emphasizes:

- individual rather than group endeavours unless a pupil chooses to work with others
- subjectivity, rather than objectivity. Creative experiences are very important for learners.
- the feeling dimension in choosing activities and experiences. The teacher is a facilitator and assists each pupil to achieve his/her goals in learning.
- the individual makes the self rather than living a predetermined life.
- to be human is to choose and choices made need to be ethical. Individuals act in a way which stresses responsibility.

Each person acts in situations in relationship to others and must be a responsible person for choices made.

A fourth philosophy to be discussed is experimentalism. Experimentalists emphasize that one cannot know ultimate reality, but each person experiences reality in a changing world in society. Experimentalism is a practical philosophy in that it deals with decision-making in every day situations. Decisions involve problem solving; absolutes do not exist. To deal with problems, individuals identify the problem, clearly. An hypothesis is developed which is a tentative solution. Information from a variety of sources need to be used with selected problems being difficult to solve, whereas others need an on the spot solution. With information, the hypothesis is tested in a life like situation, not a paper/pencil test. The consequences of each act must be noticed to reflect upon its consequences. Changes, in courses of action may need to be made in terms of possible consequences. The test reveals the quality of the hypothesis. New problems might arise in problem solving and these should have hypotheses and evaluation of the hypotheses based in information secured. One can only know what is experienced which is not based on a predetermined standard. Thus, problems and situations differ in time and place; old "tried and true" answer may not work in the new problem being considered in daily living.

There is an active and a passive side to experimentalism. The active side pertains to problem identification and solution seeking; the passive side is undergoing the consequences of choices made.

Experimentalists believe that schools should not be separated from society. Too frequently, the school curriculum stresses subject matter learnings, largely or only. The subject matter taught may have nothing to do with problems in society or with problem solving. Authentic problems, then, must be chosen for solving. There can be problem solving activities in academic subject matter when the teacher invites questions from students and these lend themselves to developing an hypotheses, information gathering, and hypotheses testing. Lecturing to students does not lend itself to this complete act of thought in problem solving.

REFERENCES

Bowyer, Carlton (1970), *Philosophical Perspectives for Education.* Glenview, Illinois: Scott, Foresman and Company.

Dewey, John (1916), *Democracy and Education.* New York: The MacMilan Company.

Ediger, Marlow (2010), *"Issues in the Social Studies,"* International Journal of Educational Research, Development and Extension, 1 (1), 43-49.

Ediger, Marlow, and D. Bhaskara Rao (2003), Philosophy and Curriculum. New Delhi, India: Discovery Publishing House.

Ediger Marlow (2006), "Testing Vs. Portfolios to Assess Achievement," OASCD Journal, 31-32.

Joyce, Bruce, *et.al.,* (1983), *The Structure of School Improvement*, New York: Longman's, Inc.

National Research Council (1995), National *Science Education Standards.* Washington, DC: National Academy Press.

Ozman, Howard A., and Samuel M. Cramer (1990), *Philosophical Foundations of Education.* Columbus, Ohio: Merrill Publishing Company.

Ray, K. W. (2006), "What Are You Thinking?" Educational Leadership, 64 (2), 58-62.

Stiggins, Richard J. (1997), Student Centered Classroom Assessment. Upper Saddle River, New Jersey: Merrill.

Thayer, V. T. (1970), Formative Ideas in American Education. New York: Dodd, Mead and Company.

Philosophical Implications in Evaluation of Learner Progress

There are diverse approaches in evaluating pupil achievement. Each of these procedures emphasize a selected philosophy of education. Teachers, school administrators, and curriculum directors need to study, analyze, and develop a sound process of evaluation. Evaluation is a possess which should be continuous and comprehensive. This is needed in order to provide feedback to the teacher as well as assist in achieving continuous progress for pupils. With higher expectations of pupil progress, it behooves educators in the school setting to match the pupils present level of attainment with what can be attained and achieved with challenging learning activities as well as with scaffolding (See Ennis, 1987).

Methods of Evaluation

An older method of appraising learner achievement is teacher observation. This approach is very salient presently. Continuously, the teacher must observe and evaluate pupils in many areas of the curriculum. This is needed to notice if pupils are achieving objectives as well as to diagnose the kinds of assistance needed by pupils. Thus, the teacher needs to utilize quality criteria in the assessment process. For example, the teacher may observe if pupils are doing better than previously in the following areas of the curriculum as well as the kinds of weaknesses exhibited which require pupil aid:

- word recognition skills and comprehension in reading
- measuring degrees of angles in mathematics
- observing carefully what transpires in a science experiment
- thinking critically and creatively in the social studies (Ediger, 2010).

The teacher's role is to teach and have pupils learn with evaluation providing information on ensuing sequential procedures of instruction. Diagnosis is a part of the evaluation process. Teacher observation needs to emphasize quality with updated standards being utilized in the evaluation process. It is immediate and assistance provided to pupils may follow as soon as diagnosis and assessment have been completed. An authentic method is used as it is direct and in context, not based on test results in and of itself, although testing may be used in conjunction with teacher observation. Testing is assessment which involves a paper/pencil test coming between the learner and what has been learned. In society, a worker is not given a test to show proficiency and quality of work performed. Rather, the actual products and demonstrated skills reveal worker effectiveness. Too frequently, testing, alone, is utilized to indicate what has been learned; however, there are a plethora of additional means of revealing achievement, such as teacher observation in

- a discussion in a purposeful activity.
- drawings and construction experiences within an ongoing unit of study.

- dramatizations and pantomimes to indicate understanding of subject matter acquired.
- experiments and demonstrations related to relevant objectives of an ensuing lesson.
- hands on activities involving doing, making, and completing (Ediger and Rao, 2003).

A second philosophy of evaluation is measurement theory with its emphasis upon testing. Testing to assess learner progress has a long history, but became very important in the early 1900s with the work of E. L. Thorndike (1874-1949). His endeavours assisted in bringing in the measurement movement with his philosophy of "Whatever exists, exists in some amount, and if it exists in some amount, it can be measured." As a result, tests were developed to measure achievement in diverse academic areas. The tests were to be aligned with the objectives of instruction and results from testing provided specific numerical results such as percentiles, age/grade equivalent scores, and stanines. Measurement theory, being even more salient presently, emphasizes objectives of instruction which are highly precise and written so that it indicates if a pupil has/has not achieved these precisely written objectives. Multiple choice test items, properly written, provides pupils with a choice from among four alternatives in selecting the correct answer. There is then a 25 per cent chance of arriving at a correct answer when guessing and harmonizes with the precision of being measurable in terms of securing information on learner progress. Measurement theory harmonizes well with the preciseness of behaviourism as a psychology of learning in that:

- it is orderly with its statement of precise objectives of instruction.
- it aligns learning activities with the stated objectives.
- its standardized tests measure how much each pupil has learned.

- its standardized tests have the same directions for test taking for all taking the test, each age/grade group has the same test items, and the same key is used to score results from testing.
- it has norms listed in the Manual when comparing pupil's test scores with those in a norm group on which the test was standardized (See Stiggins, 1997).

A third philosophy of evaluation pertains to teacher written test items. These must be valid in that they evaluate what is purported to be evaluated. Thus, a teacher written test to evaluate achievement in simple addition must evaluate simple addition and not compound subtraction, multiplication, and/or division, among others. Face validity works well here in that the teacher may write test items immediately after teaching lessons on simple addition. In addition to validity, reliability is also an important factor in written tests in that they evaluate consistently for any one pupil. Split half reliability can be assessed by an teacher. Thus odd versus even numbered test items are compared to notice if a given set of pupils ranked in the same order when comparing odd/even numbered test item test results. Alternative forms becomes more difficult to ascertain reliability in that two equivalent tests measuring the same objectives need to be in evidence to notice if a pupil scores the same for form A as compared to form B.

For each multiple choice test item written, there generally are four responses of approximately the same/similar length. Clues must not be given as to which is the correct response with each being plausible. Test items must always possess clarity to avoid pupil guessing and to determine what each pupil has learned. If essay tests are used as in problem solving, the questions should not require a factual answer nor one whereby an excessive amount of information is written. Getting at the heart of what each pupil knows and not the amount of verbiage written is important. Essay tests must involve thought, such as critical and creative thinking, in coming up with a solution such as in problem solving. Higher levels of cognition should definitely be inherent in essay test items. Matching tests, as an other approach, have more responses in column A as compared to column B so that the process of elimination may not be used in this type of test. One of the two columns should have single words or phrases so that pupils do not struggle over/with two columns, each containing a somewhat lengthy sentence. True/false test items, if used to measure learner progress must involve pupils crossing out the incorrect part of an item being false and writing in what would make the test item true. Thus guessing is minimized in using true/false test items. Completion test items might also be utilized. The test writer must be certain that adequate information is provided so that the test taker knows what is wanted. For example, the following completion test item lacks adequate wording to provide the responder with necessary information in responding: The ___ and ___ are the _ of _. The preceding may sound ridiculous, but it does make the point that essential words must be added so that the pupil responds in a meaningful manner. Then too, the blanks need to be of equal length so as not to provide clues in terms of what is wanted in the answer (See Ozman and Cramer, 1990).

Teacher written tests with proper validity and reliability might well provide needed feedback to the teacher for content inclusion in teaching and learning situations. These tests are not standardized with publication from a leading publishing company, but when clearly written and designed provide information to indicate pupil achievement. Teacher written tests might also fill in during the school year since standardized tests are given once a year, and more frequent assessments are necessary to show how well a pupil is doing in school.

A fourth philosophy in appraising pupil achievement is to use portfolios. Here, the pupil with teacher guidance chooses entries which comprise a portfolio. Thus, the learner may select the following representative products, among others, from ongoing units of study:

- summaries, outlines, and diary/log entries;
- written play parts for dramatizations, reader's theater;
- digital photos of construction and art work;
- video tapes of oral presentations, creative dramatizations, and committee endeavours;
- co-operative evaluation (pupil and teacher) in terms of clearly stated standards (See Lawson, 1999).

With the portfolio approach, pupils, the teacher, as well as parents, may view products and processes directly, not through test results. Thus, a summary may be assessed in terms of viewing it in its original form and notice learner progress as well as what needs additional attention. Involving the pupil in the conference helps him/her take note of recommendations for improvement. A test does not come between the pupil and the product for assessment purposes. Progress may be noted between earlier and later products, such as the summary being viewed. Attention may be focused upon the product and not something else. The portfolio needs to have a Table of Contents so that products to be viewed can be located readily. Portfolio contents provide opportunities for review and reflection. The learner owns the portfolio and he/she generally take much pride in viewing its contents, not only for a conference but also for becoming more conscious of the need for achievement and growth. School administrators and the curriculum director should also take time to assess portfolios (See Rover and Feldman,1984).

Conclusion

Evaluation is an integral part of teaching. Feedback from evaluation guides instruction with the best curriculum possible being provided for each pupil. Salient knowledge, skills, and attitudes need to be developed within carefully selected objectives of instruction.

REFERENCES

Ediger, Marlow, and D. Bhaskara Rao (2003), *Philosophy and Curriculum*. New Delhi, India: Discovery Publishing House.

Ediger, Marlow, and D. Bhaskara Rao (2010), *Effective School Curriculum*. New Delhi, India: Discovery Publishing House.

Ennis, R. H. (1987), *A Taxonomy of Critical Thinking Disposition and Abilities*. J. B. Baron and R. J. Sternberg, (Eds.), Teaching Thinking Skills: *Theory and Practice*. New York: Freeman, 9-26.

Ozman Howard, and Samuel Cramer (1990), Philosophical Foundations of Education. Columbus, Ohio: Merrill Publishing Company.

Lawson, T. J. (1999), *"Assessing Critical Thinking as a Learning Outcome for Psychology Majors,"* Teaching of Psychology, 26(1), 207-208.

Royer, James M., and Robert S. Feldman (1984), *Educational Applications and Theory.* New York: Alfred A.Knopf, Inc.

Stiggins, Richard J. (1997), Student Centered Classroom Assessment. Upper Saddle River, New Jersey: Merrill.

Philosophical Implications in Selecting Objectives of Instruction

Teachers, curriculum directors, and school administrators need to study and appraise objectives for pupil achievement in terms of philosophical implications in order to improve the quality of objectives for pupil attainment. Mandated objectives also leave leeway for additional, quality objectives in the school curriculum. Mandated objectives are stated quite precisely and in measurable terms. Either pupils do/do not achieve them as a result of learning activities provided in the school/classroom setting. Additional philosophical schools of thought also might well serve to enrich the learnings provided for pupils. Philosophy of mandated objectives will be analyzed first in this manuscript (Ediger and Rao, 2003).

Objectives of Instruction

Measurably stated objectives with accompanying aligned tests represent a popular approach presently in teaching and learning situations. Mandated objectives, be they district state, or nation wide tend to emphasize the use of standardized tests which should possess accompanying objectives for teachers to use in gauging teaching and learning in the direction of measurably stated ends. These precise objectives lend themselves to having aligned learning experiences chosen by teachers in the classroom. With multiple choice test items on the standardized tests taken by pupils, machine scoring may be used to score large numbers of tests. Test results may then reveal, numerically, a percentile, age/grade equivalent, and/or stannic for each pupil. The results may also indicate class, school, district, state, and national comparisons for a news media report card evaluation.

Mandated objectives stress Stimulus/Response theory of learning in that there is a learner connection to each knowledge item acquired. The stimulus then brings on a pupil response with previously acquired content which bridges the new learning or knowledge taught Multiple choice test items, for example, may have a stem and the test taker locates the correct answer from four detractors, *e.g.* Which is the capital city of Austria? A) Berlin; B) Vienna; C) Budapest; D) Prague. There are no clues given as to the correct response. The test taker is to connect/associate the stimulus (Austria) with the response (Vienna). Stimulus/ response theory of learning has a long history with E. L Thorndike (1874-1949) stating that "whatever exists, exists in some amount, and if it exists in some amount, it can be measured." Many standardized tests were developed in Thorndike's day and later to measure pupil achievement in different academic disciplines. These tests contained:

- the same directions to be given to test takers, prior to taking the standardized test.
- the same test items for each age or grade level.
- the same key for test scoring (Ediger, 2010).

Present day standardized tests still follow the above named standards and are used for accountability purposes; they are used once each school year. Teachers are then held accountable for pupils doing well on the test in order to be promoted to the next grade level in grades three through eight. Also, an exit test must be taken and passed to receive a high school diploma.

Decision-making philosophy represents a second school of thought in the school and classroom setting. Individual decision-making, for example, may be emphasized with individualized reading. Here, an adequate number of library books on different genre need to be available. They also must be on diverse reaching levels to provide for individual differences. The teacher needs to introduce new titles at selected intervals. An attractive bulletin board display assists pupils to choose reading materials. The learner then chooses an interesting library book to read. The selection is up to the individual with the teacher helping those who cannot decide. The teacher monitors the classroom reading environment and guides learners who need assistance with word pronunciation. The library books chosen should help to engage pupils in desiring to read. After the completion of reading a library book, the pupil has a conference to indicate comprehension and word recognition growth. The learner chooses which selection from the library book to read aloud to the teacher as well as being encouraged to raise questions for discussion during the conference. The teacher records information and dates it making comparisons with the next conference. Growth and achievement are to be noted within each conference.

Individualized reading programmes are based upon:

- pupils vary from each other in reading skills and knowledge interests which call for library books of different levels of complexity and subject matter content.
- pupils need to choose in order to select library books sequentially which meet personal needs.
- pupil interest is a powerful factor in learning to read proficiently.

- pupils possess diverse purposes in choosing library books to read (Ediger, 2010).

Basal textbook use represents a third approach in a philosophical procedure in curriculum development. Here in the school or district setting, teachers, among other professionals, have selected a basal series of textbooks in terms of desired criteria. The textbook then, becomes the foundational setting in selecting objectives of instruction. The accompanying Manual contains a list of objectives for teachers to emphasize in teaching. Also, objectives may need additions/deletions, depending upon the philosophy of the school. Thus, the teacher may rigidly follow the Manual or add/modify objectives.

If objectives are added/modified, they serve to broaden the scope of what is taught, as well as possibly increasing objectives which deal with higher level cognitive objectives. Generally textbook content is highly condensed and needs a wider scope such as in the social studies where the Middle East area of the world receives a narrow focus in textbook content. The nation of Jordan might receive short shrift. Also, a social science discipline such as sociology may need to be incorporated to provide a model for how culture affects human behaviour.

Relying upon the basal text for teaching pupils may make for a rigid, formal curriculum. Whereas, a teacher must be creative in using a Manual and other methods of teaching to meet the needs of individual learners. Too frequently, too, large group class as a whole instruction predominates. To provide for individual differences, small group and individual tasks must also be in the offing. Objectives must stress what is meaningful, interesting, possess purpose, and challenge. Basal textbooks have certain advantages in teaching use in that:

- there is a structure for teachers to follow which then may be broadened in scope by the teacher.

- the Manual presents teaching suggestions for consideration and new ideas may also be incorporated to provide for individual differences.
- they are written by specialists in the field (See Stiggins, 1997).

A fourth philosophy of education to emphasize is constructivism. Constructivists do not believe in the testing movement. Rather, pupils construct their own knowledge as a lesson or unit of study progresses. The role of the teacher is to encourage and assist pupils to achieve sequentially. Here, the teacher does not lecture nor tell correct answers when pupils have questions. Rather, the teacher helps pupils to find answers to their questions. If, for example, a pupil has a question, the teacher may raise questions(s) leading the pupil to an answer. The learner is control of the curriculum and sequences his/her own knowledge and skills. Thus, if a pupil or committee is working on a project, they may proceed with a minimal amount of assistance. The project possesses a purpose since pupils have in inward desire to pursue. Careful planning is needed to develop the project. As pupils follow through with the plans, they largely work independently with minimal teacher guidance. Sequence resides within the mind of the pupil, not the teacher, although the latter carefully observes learner achievement to provide encouragement when deemed necessary. Teacher observation is a major procedure to use in evaluating pupil progress with assistance given as needed to make for continual progress. The pupil eventually develops criteria and appraises his/her project in terms of these desired criteria. Constructivists emphasize the following tenets:

- pupils being independent, not teacher dependent in learning.
- pupils being active learners, not passive recipients of knowledge.
- the role of the teacher is not to be "the sage on the stage," but rather a helper in assisting pupils to achieve objectives of instruction.

- pupils are actively involved in ordering their very own experiences.
- self evaluation by pupils is salient with teacher observation also being involved.
- pupils have much input into developing the curriculum (See Gardner, 1993).

There are differences in the four philosophies discussed. Each has its own generalizations with the teacher having different roles and responsibilities. Pupils also are perceived to have differences in relating to the curriculum (See Shanklin and Rhodes, 1989). The following then are issues as a educators continue to develop/modify a new philosophy:

- is the learner a passive or active being in securing knowledge and skills?
- who should have ownership of the curricula, the teacher/ and or the pupil?
- should the teacher or the pupil basically sequence (earnings?
- what is the role of academic subject matter in learning?
- should objectives be predetermined or should they arise within a lesson or unit of study?
- how and by whom should pupil progress be assessed?

Teachers and others in the school setting must appraise the objectives, learning opportunities, and the evaluation section of the curriculum to notice what might be modified or changed. The best of each philosophical school of thought needs to be utilized in formulating the curriculum (De Roche and Kostelny, 2006).

REFERENCES

De Roche, and Susan Kostelny (2006), *"An Adventure in Problem Based Learning,"* Phi Delta Kappan, 87 (9), 708.

Ediger, Marlow, and D. Bhaskara Rao (2003), *Philosophy and Curriculum.* New Delhi, India: Discovery Publishing House.

Ediger, Marlow (2010), *"Sequence in the Social Studies,"* Edutracks, 9 (11), 9-10.

Ediger, Marlow (2010), *"Issues in Social Studies,"* International Journal of Educational Research, Development, and Extension, 1 (1), 43-49.

Gardner, Howard (1993), *Multiple Intelligences: Theory into Practice.* New York: Basic Books.

Shanklin, N. L, and L.K. Rhodes (1989), *''Comprehension Instruction as Sharing and Extending,"* The Reading Teacher, 42 (5), 496-500.

Stiggins, Richard (1997), *Student Centered Classroom Assessment.* Upper Saddle River, New Jersey: Merrill.

Psychology in Curriculum Development

Teachers, Supervisors, and School Administrators Desire to Assist Pupils to Attain Optimally. The psychology of learning certainly may help in this area and is designed to do so. There are selected principles of learning which when used might guide pupils to achieve objectives of instruction. Pupils differ from each other in a variety of ways such as interests possessed, purposes perceived, attitudes acquired, as well as values developed. Thus, individual differences among learners must be provided for in the classroom. Using the same methods of instruction, the same materials of instruction, and having the same expectations for each is not realistic. Rather, the teacher must adapt methods used which are suitable to assisting learner achievement and progress. Materials of instruction need to engage pupils in the learning process, while achievement expectations for each pupil's achievement must be high but reasonable. Teachers need to be well prepared for each day of teaching and incorporate salient tenets of educational psychology. Securing the interests of pupils is of utmost importance.

Disconnected from studying and attending will not maximize learner progress. The teacher needs to secure and maintain intense pupil interest in ongoing lessons and units of study. He/she must observe pupils rather continuously to notice if adequate pupil concentration is there. Each educational psychologist to be discussed focused upon a selected psychology which, if applied, should aid pupil progress (Ediger, 2007).

Relevant Psychologies of Education

There are educational psychologists who have contributed much to curriculum development and teaching/learning situations. The influence of their thinking and research is quite evident in what is being emphasized presently. Behaviourism as a psychology of learning stresses the saliency of measuring pupil learning in precise numerical terms, such as percentite, age/grade equivalent, and stanine results. B. F Skinner (1902-1986) was very prominent in advocating measuring pupil achievement and not leaving subjective judgements of learner achievement up to the teacher. Dr. Skinner advocated Stimulus/Response theory in his written programmed materials. In using programmed learning, pupils rarely made mistakes in a tightly knitted sequence. Here, pupils, for example, read a sentence or two and then responded to a multiple choice test item. If the response was correct, reinforcement was in evidence; rewarding correct answers is known as operant conditioning. Thus, Skinner placed the stress upon the correctness of a response, rather than the stimulus. Earlier, Pavlov, Russian physiologist in his experiments with dogs, emphasized the stimulus. Changing the stimulus brought on a different response. Thus, a dog was conditioned to salivate with the sound of a bell only whereas the unconditioned stimulus (UCS) such as meat caused the dog to salivate. The site of meat and the sounding of a bell (conditioned stimulus) together, ultimately lead to the dog salivating solely through the sounding of the bell. With operant conditioning, Dr. Skinner brought to the attention of educators the importance of properly ordered materials of instruction as well as building the self-concept due to learner success in achievement. Testing then becomes very important; generally standardized tests are favoured with those containing high validity and reliability. This can be noticed with mandated testing which provide standards for pupils being promoted to the next grade level, if a passing score is received (See Donahue, 2000).

Mandated testing advocates also use behaviourism as a model for prescribed learning. Standardized tests used are aligned with the measurably stated objectives and are written, generally, by specialists in each academic area. The classroom teacher selects learning activities which assist pupils to achieve the stated objectives of instruction. Operant conditioning within behaviourist psychology in programmed learning emphasizes a high success rate in each pupil's learning whereas mandated testing stresses sorting pupils in terms of those passing/failing the test, as well as making comparisons among different classrooms, schools, school systems, and states (See Gore, 1993). The following are major summary statements pertaining to behaviourism as a psychology of learning including mandated testing and operant conditioning:

- precision is emphasized with measurably stated objectives
- tests are aligned with the objectives of instruction
- test results from pupils generally are quantifiable
- tests usually consist of multiple choice items
- machine scoring is used with mandated testing in which many students take the tests on the state or national levels
- pupil, classroom, school system, and state achievement levels of learners may be compared to notice successful and failing schools.

Jean Piaget, Swiss educator who studied children for over fifty years, came up with a maturation theory of learning. What children can learn depends upon their stage of maturity, dependent upon age levels. He came up with the following approximate levels of maturity in learning:

- psychomotor stage, ages birth to age 18 months. Here, infants learned from objects which move such as clatter balls fastened to a crib. The young child might then move the spheres attached to soft rod. White doing this, the eyes of the infant watches the movement and hears the sounds involved. Many toys that can be held by/for the child are then used to shaking with the attending different noises. The gradual movement, soft noise, and the feeling of the toys make for learning.
- preoperational stage, eighteen months to seven years. Here, the child sees one variable when making comparisons among objects. Thus, a glass of water as compared to pouring that same water into a taller thinner container makes the youngster believe that the taller, thinner container has more water as compared to the original glassful, even though the water was poured from one container to the next directly in front of the observer. Perceiving one variable only is quite typical of these children, ages 18 months to seven years, as they continue to learn.
- stage of concrete operations, ages seven to eleven. Here, the learner needs real objects to learn from as the abstract leanings are being emphasized. Thus, a small model horse is necessary when reading the related abstract word. The school may not possess all the needed models, but it is good for the learner to associate the concrete with the abstract. Reasoning skills are starting to enter into the teaching and learning situation with further and indepth skills added in sequential achievement.

- stage of abstract thought, beginning at age, eleven and twelve in which children increasingly possess the ability to problem solve notice variables, as well as engage in critical and creative thinking without referring directly to concrete materials of instruction.

Jean Piaget, then, emphasized the saliency of maturation in teaching and learning situations. Abraham Maslow developed a humanistic theory of learning whereby the child and his/her environment need careful consideration in the curriculum. Maslow, first of all, believed the physiological needs of children need attention. Thus, adequate nutrition, good shelter/homes, and clothing need to be taken care of. These are prerequisites to developing the desire to learn in school. Second, pupils need to have safety needs taken care of. Abusive situations and harassment should not be experienced by children. Achievement comes about if pupils feel secure from all alarm. Third, all like to feel they belong in a class or school. Being an isolate and not being accepted makes for uncomfortable situations. Teachers need to assist pupils in becoming a part of the group setting. Fourth, esteem needs must be met; pupils like to feel successful and be recognized for achievement. Pupils, no doubt, do not like school due to the lack of recognition for deeds and acts. Eventually, dropping out of school may occur. When alt these preceding needs have been met, pupils are ready to achieve more optimally.

Jerome Bruner viewed subject matter as being main ingredients in learning. He emphasized that pupils achieve structural content in different academic disciplines. The structural ideas may be identified by subject matter specialists such as a professors of history identifying key ideas in history; these main ideas are then available to teachers who assist pupils in achievement. Thus, teachers must meticulously identify major generalizations of learner attainment. So often trivia is emphasized such as irrelevant names, dates, and places, and this may be avoided or minimized with helping pupils acquire structural content. The structure provides the framework of an academic discipline upon which related subject matter may be built Learning opportunities need to emphasize pupil's attaining inductive these structural ideas. The teacher must possess a good knowledge of subject matter to help pupils learn content, using discovery methods of teaching. He/she encourages and assists whenever necessary. The structure of knowledge approach used in teaching has the following advantages:

- assistance is available to teachers in selecting what is salient for pupils to learn;
- teachers may focus upon teaching what is relevant, not the mundane and insignificant;
- pupils are excited in learning subject matter by discovery rather than lecture or telling methods;
- pupils may work as academicians do using the same tools and approaches;
- teams might well meet up with the same/similar structural ideas as different units of study are taught;
- evaluation may consist of pupils achieving and attaching meaning to identified key, structural ideas.

Daniel Goleman (1995) focuses upon Emotional Intelligence (EI). He emphasizes the importance of psychological factors which might well create problems at school and the work place. A worker, for example, may have know how to succeed at these places, but have difficulties in getting atong with others. Negative feelings and attitudes get in the way of being proficient. Goleman states the EQ may be more salient than IQs possessed. Teachers in the classroom notice the following situations:

- pupils who are isolates and seemingly fail to be able to connect with others
- pupils who pout when they do not their way and might frequently feel sorry for themselves

- pupils who disturb others and keep them from studying
- pupils, individually, who roam around the classroom and cannot settle down to learn
- pupils who like to entertain and want to be class clowns which disrupt discussions
- pupils who are quick to pick fights on the playground
- pupils who harass others in diverse ways (Ediger, 2010).

There are pupils who become angry soon at the least provocation. This is shown as consistent behaviour. Anger management is important since an angry individual may do many things which are regrettable later on. This has ruined a person's life. Teachers need to view and diagnose those who have problems with anger, among other forms of unapproved behaviours, and assist all pupils to be accepted by others as well as be well adjusted. They need to emphasize committee work whereby each does his/her fair share of work as well as working harmoniously with others. Good human relations and social development of each pupil is significant. Individuals must know and manage their emotions, as well as know the feelings of others. Social skills need developing and using when relating to others. Non-verbal skills need honing such as having appropriate facial expressions, tone of voice, and postures/gestures.

Howard Gardner (1993) emphasized multiple intelligences theory in providing for individual differences in a classroom. Thus, more than one intelligence (IQ) is possessed by learners in a school setting. Teachers need to provide for pupils of different intelligences. Thus, the following, among others, are important to consider in teaching and learning situations:

- verbal intelligence such as learner experiences in reading and writing activities in diverse curriculum areas. In gathering information, these pupils achieve much in terms of reading subject matter content.

- logical intelligence in which learners do well in using logic as is true in mathematics as well as in other academic disciplines.
- musical/rhythmical as in writing lyrics and putting these to music to reveal what has been learned. This activity may be correlated with any facet of unit teaching by putting that which has been learned to music. Rhythmical experiences, also, are salient as in folk dances related to social studies units of instruction.
- intrapersonal experiences whereby the student prefers to work by the self and does well in achieving objectives of instruction.
- interpersonal intelligence whereby the pupil prefers to work collectively in committees to attain and accomplish in ongoing lessons/units of study.
- bodily/kinesthetic intelligence stresses the importance of manual dexterity as well as eye hand co-ordination. There are pupils who do well, for example, in constructing models, science equipment, and engaging in the project method. Athletic endeavours also stress bodily/kinesthetic intelligence.
- Scientific intelligence whereby the pupils shows high capabilities in objective thinking. Objective thinking is stressed in all curriculum areas, and especially in science.
- artistic intelligence in which the child shows proficiency in creative thinking in using space to reveal what has been produced in art work. When viewing art products in national museums, the viewer is fascinated with the following: media used and blended to produce a product, unique interpretations used by the artist, perseverance which went into completing a work of art, as well as beauty expressed by the artist.

Conclusion

Teachers, supervisors, and principals might gain much from a study of leading educational psychologists and their beliefs and ideas with the intent of applying selected major generalizations in improving the curriculum. Thus, the following are salient:

- Skinner with his emphasis upon learner success when activities are sequenced appropriately.
- Piaget with stress placed upon stages of pupils maturing properly before learning opportunities are implemented.
- Maslow with his emphasis on meeting pupil needs holistically.
- Bruner with relevancy placed upon teaching significant subject matter.
- Goleman with importance placed upon developing well socially and emotionally.
- Gardner with placing saliency upon abilities possessed by individuals and providing for important differences.

REFERENCES

Donahue, P. (2000), *"Evaluating Teaching,"* ADE Bulletin, 126 (1), 46-47.

Ediger, Marlow (2010), *"Constructivism and the Social Studies,"* Edutracks, 9 (7), 13-15.

Ediger, Marlow (2007), *"Learning Activities in the Curriculum,"* College Student Journal, 41 (4), 967-969.

Gardner, Howard (1983), *Frames of Mind: The Theory of Multiple Intelligences.* New York: Basic Books.

Goleman, Daniel (1995), *Emotional Intelligence; Why it Can Matter More Than IQ.* New York: Bantam Books.

Gore, G. R. (1993), *"What is Good Teaching?*[1] Physics Teacher, 31 (8), 482.

Psychology in Selection of Objectives of Instruction

It is of utmost importance in choosing vital objectives for pupil attainment. What is salient to teach should be contained in these relevant ends. Objectives have changed in time but not always for the good of the learner. A study of important objectives is necessary in order to choose the best for pupils. There, of course, is subjectivity in the selecting of objectives. Educators are human beings who choose what pupils are to learn. They use reason, societal trends, recommendations from learned societies, academicians, and curriculum specialists in making these choices.

Many statements of objectives have been written and published to indicate what is considered salient.

Objectives and the Learner

An important set of progressive objectives was published by the Commission to Reorganize Secondary Education, of the National Education Association (USA) in 1918 (See Bibliography). These are equally salient for the elementary school level. The categories were the following:

- health. Proper nutrition, exercise, suitable clothing, meeting medical and dental needs, among others.
- command of fundamental processes. This includes vital subject matter learnings as well as skills needed in school and in society.
- worthy home membership. These learnings which include knowledge and skills which may be integrated into many units of study and are certainly needed in an era of recession, economically, which affects any involved family.
- ethical character. One must learn to deal fairly and truthfully in relating to others.
- vocational competence. This objective emphasizes being interested in and becoming knowledgeable about relevant jobs, careers, and professions.
- citizenship. The person develops those attitudes as well as knowledge, and skills to function well as a member in society.
- worthy use of leisure time. The individual finds positive ways to use spare time wisely.

The above Seven Cardinal Principles provide a broad framework in educating the whole child. These objectives represented, indeed, a progressive education curriculum. The total development of the child is emphasized and extends well beyond acquiring subject matter content. Holism in the curriculum is definitely in evidence. Each broad goal may be changed to specific objectives for teaching and learning situations in many units of instruction.

The National Education Association, again, issued a set of broad educational objectives with four broad, major areas of concern developed by the Educational Policies Commission in 1938:

- an educated person in school and social setting
- human relationships in the family, community, and larger social setting.

- economic well being as a consumer and producer.
- quality citizenship as a worthy member in society.

Subgoals are stated in this report for each of the above four asterisked areas (Educational Policies Commission, 1938). The broadly stated objectives as well as the sub-objectives may be stated as relevant ends for pupil attainment and, if relevant, become inherent in daily lesson plans. In selected cases, the 1918 and the 1938 statement of objectives are important today and can be updated with included statements of objectives in vogue presently.

There are objectives, presently, for pupil achievement which are mandated and have aligned tests. Pupils take these standardized tests once a year to reveal progress. Thus, in grades three through eight, pupils are tested in reading and mathematics, as well as in science. Pupils need to pass these tests to be promoted to the next higher grade level, as in the No Child Left Behind (NCLB) law of 2002 (USA). High school students also need to pass an exit test for graduation purposes. These tests are written by specialists and are then available in different states in the union. Each state has their own standardized test, making it difficult to make comparisons among test scores in comparing one state with another. The results are printed and announced in the media, being referred to as the nation's report card. Comparisons are also made among school districts and within schools. Competition is emphasized here in having school districts as well as individual schools meet challenging standards. Schools also need to meet Adequate Yearly Progress (AYP) so that students may achieve "proficiency" by 2014. There are difficulties involved in using NCLB standards:

- the scope of the curriculum is too narrow with pupils being tested in reading, mathematics, and science.
- pupils are tested once a year only, to indicate if they should be promoted.

- multiple choice test items are generally used to test pupils, making it difficult to evaluate higher levels of learner cognition.
- knowledge and skills objectives predominate, leaving out measuring quality attitudes of pupils.
- salient objectives are omitted as in good human relations and caring for others (Ediger, 2003).

For domain specific frameworks in developing broadly stated purposes, the National Council for the Social Studies (NCSS, 1992) developed the following themes, with elaboration by the author, as organizing strands for social studies programmes:

(1) culture. This theme brings in the academic disciplines of anthropology and sociology. The society in which people live affects human behaviour such as languages spoken, foods eaten, patterns in recreation, types of music available, and means of transportation.

(2) time, continuity, and change. In units stressing history, learners should attain objectives emphasizing how changes occur in society such as the Great Depression of the 1930s and how the different levels of government dealt with grave problem areas.

(3) people, places, and environment. Among other things, pupils need to learn about the kinds of occupations and jobs individuals/groups perform within a specific geographical region and how natural resources are used/preserved.

(4) individual development and identity. Here, pupils among other, items, need to acquire knowledge and skills pertaining to human growth and maturation, as well as what makes for personal achievement.

(5) power, authority and governance. Understandings must be acquired pertaining to different levels of government in political science such as local, state, and federal levels as well as how they are affected, as citizens, by these different levels of governance.

(6) production, consumption, and distribution. Pupils learn about goods and services produced for human use. Goods and services are distributed through a long list of processes in order to reach where they are needed.

(7) science, technology, and society. Objectives in science need to be carefully selected so that pupils might learn to think objectively and scientifically. Science then provides necessary content for life, living, and technological advances such as use of cyber space, computers, and other inventions which assist in providing for quality endeavours.

(8) individuals, groups, and institutions. The human being and membership in groups such as the family, clubs, organizations, and as a member in society must be salient in the curriculum.

(9) global connections. People, nations, and cultures interact in an era of rapid transportation and communication systems.

(10) civic ideals and practices. Active participation in the community by citizens needs to be emphasized as in "no person is an island unto itself."

Each of the above structure may be incorporated into ongoing units of study. They might also be planned as an entire unit. The Task Force for NCSS (2010) has also produced standards for each of these ten areas. Thus, for example, pertaining to civic ideals and practices, the following sample of knowledge goals is significant: Learners will understand:

- the theme of civic ideals and practices helps us to know how we can have influence on how people live and act together.
- concepts such as individual dignity, fairness, freedom, the common good, rule of law, civic life, rights and responsibilities.

- key practices in a democratic society include civic participation based on studying community issues, planning, decision-making, voting, and co-operating to promote civic ideals.
- democratic ideals and practices are often represented in excerpts from contemporary and historical sources, quotations, and stories.
- the importance of gathering information as the basis for informed civic action.

These more specific objectives may be stated behaviourally so that achievement can be measured. However, selected objectives may need to be broadly stated due to the difficulties of writing civics objectives very precisely.

Objectives need careful study and revision, when warranted. Periodically, new objectives need to be incorporated, but this is to be done only when definite needs exist, not for the sake of doing so. Society changes and so does what is salient to teach. Change is one of the facts of life and a curricula must be relevant for each pupil. Outdated curricula make for learners who will lack motivation to attain vital objectives. They must perceive a purpose for learning so that reasons are in evidence for achievement. Outdated objectives have made for situations whereby pupils wonder why these leanings are taught. Interest certainly will then be lacking when objectives are irrelevant and pupils fail to be actively involved in learning. Active engagement is needed with interesting objectives for pupils to achieve. When supervising university student teachers, the writer, too frequently, has noticed learners who are turned off in achieving. It is no wonder when viewing objectives for lessons and units of study being taught. Teachers, supervisors, and school administrators must observe to see if pupils are fully involved in what is being taught. Lessons and units of study need changes when pupils see little/no purpose in learning. From purposeless to purposeful objectives are modifications which must be made in any academic discipline. Faculty meetings, diverse forms of inservice education, as well as conferences must focus upon developing salient objectives for learner attainment. Faculty members and school administrators have as an obligation to continually seek the best objectives possible for pupils. The objectives become targets for teachers to aim toward in teaching and learning situations. Room is left for learner input into curriculum development (See Hedin and Conderman, 2010).

Constructivism

Constructivism as a psychology of teaching and learning emphasizes pupils establishing what is reasonable within ongoing activities. Thus, there objectives which pupils have in mind as they engage in learning. As pupils learn, they continually modify what is being accepted as being correct. With these modifications, pupils individually are more accurate in ultimate content and skills secured. The focus is upon the pupil achieving inductively. Lecture definitely is not a part of instructional procedures. Instead, the pupil learns through inquiry, not by the teacher aiming toward predetermined objectives. If pupils have questions and problems, the teacher assists in finding answers by asking questions of the learner which lead to the correct answer. The teacher must have a good subject matter knowledge base to use inquiry methods of teaching. Pupils acquire and form their own knowledge and skills in context, but these concepts are modified as needed. This is not anarchy, but it is the way pupils learn. Each one fashions his/her own truth and then modifies within a contextual setting.

Teacher observation is used to appraise progress. When observing learner achievement, he/she notices how energetic pupils are in learning and the desire that exists to achieve. Motivation to learn is also observed with learner interests in mind. The interest factor is highly salient in learning since this does determine the direction of learning and how to channel intrinsic interests. Learning by discovery makes for enthusiasm and excitement in achieving and yet measurement of achievement is not emphasized; rather the pupil provides impetus in sequential learnings. The teacher is a resource person and encourages pupil achievement.

Conclusion

In the selection of objectives, the following criteria need to be followed:

- they need to be achievable with high expectations involved, but success in learning for the pupil is salient
- scaffolding must be used in certain situations so that optimal achievement is possible
- behaviourism emphasizes the use of measurably stated objectives in teaching whereas constructivism stresses the use of open ended goals
- measurably stated objectives may provide impetus for learning in that pupils realize that these need achieving in order to be promoted to the next grade level whereas constructivism stresses that learning is its own reward.

REFERENCES

Commission on the Reorganization of Secondary Education (1918). Washington, DC: Department of the Interior, Bureau of Education Bulletin, #35.

Ediger, Marlow (2003), *"Teacher Involvement to Evaluate Achievement,"* Education, 12 (1),137-142.

Educational Policies Commission (1938), *The Purposes of Education in American Democracy.* Washington, DC: National Education Association.

Hedin, Laura R., and Greg Conderman (2010), *"Teach Students to Comprehend Through Rereading,"* The Reading Teacher, 63 (7), 556-565.

NCSS (1992), *Expectations of Excellence: Curriculum Standards for the Social Studies.* Washington DC: National Council for the Social Studies.

NCSS Task Force (2010), *"The Revised Social Studies Standards,"* as stated in Social Education, 74 (4), 204-209.

CHAPTER 10

Learning Opportunities to Achieve Objectives

Learning opportunities need to focus upon the learner and what is relevant to study. Learning opportunities should be varied to provide for individual needs, interests, and styles of learning. Too frequently, a single kind of activity is provided such as use of basal textbooks in teaching and this fails to stimulate many pupils in learning. Each learner must be fully involved in achieving as much as possible. Varying the kinds of activities may help to involve learners in the learning process. Thus, selected pupils may learn more from abstract materials such as reading and writing experiences whereas others need more of concrete activities involving hands on approaches including doing, constructing, and making (See Leddy, 2010).

Learning Activities and the Pupil

There are diverse classification systems pertaining to the topic of learning activities. The well known educator Johann Friedrich Pestalozzi (1746-1826) emphasized the use of objects in teaching. Presently, this is called the concrete phase of instruction. Thus, Pestalozzi in his object lessons had pupils view and discuss real objects, models, and in taking excursions, in relating reading instruction to reality. In his day, pupils tended to memorize and parrot back answers pertaining to what was read. Understanding or meaning was then omitted in the learning process. Additional Pestalozzian examples emphasized looking at an object such as a model of a bird when writing about this topic. In science, when pupils studied insects, they would look at insects during an excursion and view things like the head, thorax, and abdomen. In addition to objects (the concrete phase of learning today), Pestalozzi stressed a well known principle of learning and that being for teachers to go from the known to the unknown. In his day, what was learned by pupils might well have been disconnected with what was known. This was certainly in evidence with the thinking of Puritan education in Colonial America in the 1630s when the Horn Book, made up of one page was memorized by pupils in terms of its contents, consisting of the upper and lower cases of the alphabet, the Lord's Prayer, as well as the Benediction (Cremin, 1977).

With pupils achieving objectives whereby known subject matter and skills are used as foundational aims in moving to achieving ensuing goals, quality sequence might well be emphasized. The learner perceives relationships then between the new and the previously acquired knowledge and skills. It is also good to have pupils relate the subject matter and abilities to their very own lives. This breeds more familiarity to the child's repertoire in attaining ensuing objectives of instruction. Pupils may also realize connectedness between and among curriculum areas in an integrated curriculum. Perceiving ideas as being unrelated hinders the recall of content as well as in retention. Thus, for example in discussions, pupils with teacher assistance may be better able to elaborate on ideas being discussed as well as to see a horizontal relationship with other academic disciplines. Discussions, too, should guide learners to do indepth understandings of subject matter and ideas discussed. Critical thinking and analyzing content makes for higher levels of cognition and should help pupils to deal better with problems faced in school and in society. New ideas, also, need to be forthcoming and creativity may well be stressed in discussions as well as when pupils work by themselves. In other words, good discussions may lead to pupil achievement in a variety of ways and improve the quality of sequence in learning. Then too, sometimes, pupils may not understand a concept, but with scaffolding the gap between where the learner is and where the teacher would desire him/her to be can be eliminated or minimized through scaffolding (See Shepherd and Ragan, 1982).

Concerns about sequence in pupil learning might well go back to the philosophy/psychology of education as perceived by Johann Friedrich Herbart (1776-1841). In his laboratory school, Herbart trained teachers to include five steps of instruction within the implemented lesson plan. These were the following:

- preparation. This involves readiness factors such as reviewing what was studied previously so the learner may understand the new content presented.
- presentation. Here, the teacher presents the new subject matter as planned in the lesson plan.
- association. The teacher assists pupils to connect the new with the old. Pupils need to perceive relationships.
- generalization. Pupils are lead to form conclusions and broad ideas covering the step of association.
- use. Learners are to use the subject matter gleaned in a variety of ways so that it is not forgotten (See Knight, 1951).

The above asterisked steps of preparation followed by presentation certainly did emphasize sequence in learning (See Tiedt, 1982). Thus, the order of learning experiences from the previous learnings to the new were related. The step of association emphasized that learnings not be isolated but connected to each other. Developing one or more generalizations from the association, also, stressed combining ideas into a totality. Unrelated facts were not stressed in teaching. Using what has been acquired made it possible that learnings be practical and applicable to many situations. Thus, improving sequence has been stressed from Herbart's day or earlier to the present.

Diverse kind of thinking are vital in today's learning activities for pupils. In school and in society, individuals must be able to think to function well in the many responsibilities which life has to offer. Absorbing facts is not adequate since these lack relevancy by themselves in the identification and solving of problems (Dewey, 1916). There are several kinds of thinking which might well be integrated into all curriculum areas. Thus, critical thought is salient in that one analyzes fact from fiction, relevant from irrelevant content, as well as accurate from inaccurate content. After analyzing, one has a better chance of using the best information possible in life's endeavours. Then too, pupils need to come up with unique and novel ideas. Why? There are situations which require newness of ideas since the older approaches have not worked. Novel ideas have also made for progress in life. Thus in medical practices, the length of human life has been extended through improved pharmaceuticals, surgical methods, preventative medicine, x-rays, among others. The world of work has been made more pleasant with machines, automation, and technology.

Transportation is more rapid including the use of plane, train, and automobiles. Farms are more productive than ever with commercial fertilizers, better farm machines with air conditioned cabs, and automation. Automation is certainly in evidence with cage layers in rows in hen houses. Mash (feed) goes along a conveyor belt in troughs to keep food, available constantly as well as water flowing, also in troughs, by gravity flow in front of each cage of layers. Eggs are collected as they come on the conveyor belt, with the flip of a switch, toward the end of the long row where they are packed automatically into boxes to be placed in a cool room until a trucker comes and picks them up to go to a distribution center. From the distribution center, the eggs are placed in cartons, through automation, with minimal human effort and then taken to super-markets.

An early educator, emphasizing creativity in teaching, was Friedrich Wilhelm Froebel (1782-1842) in his kindergarten in Germany. In what he called "occupations" whereby the young child developed illustrations of different kinds as well as made other creative products. Froebel also used "mother play songs" in which children would spontaneously dramatize what was being sung. Froebel encouraged much spontaneity among pupils. In his day, schools were quite authoritarian in strictness of discipline and in pupil's memorizing content; he was a true reformer. Play was emphasized as learning experiences for children rather than idle behaviour. Presently, creativity is stressed in the following kinds of learning opportunities for children, based on their developmental level:

- creative dramatizations pertaining to subject matter studied.
- reader's theater presentations whereby each reader may portray a person, among others, by using voice inflection, appropriate stress and pitch in providing oral content.
- project methods in which pupils plan and do, in completing a model, a scene, or construction item.
- written work including rhymed and unrhymed verse, essays, stories, conclusions and summaries.
- developing games, puzzles, murals, and bulletin board displays (Ediger and Rao, 2010).

Pupils may also be encouraged to reveal creativity during discussions and seminars. Thus, original, novel, and unique ideas are being presented. One of the most valuable skills, involving creativity that any one can obtain is problem solving. In the school setting, there are human relations and discipline problems to solve. These require effort, creativity as well as plans which remedy deficiencies. These certainly can be complex in their solving, and new procedures and approaches must be garnered. When solving problems, the individual/group must always look at the consequences of a tentative solution. The consequences of an act can be more favourable if these are evaluated thoroughly in terms of desired standards, prior to their implementation.

Contrasting Modern versus Traditional Approaches in Teaching

The modern teacher respects learner ideas and invites contributions from pupils into teaching and learning situations, whereas the traditional teacher does much lecturing and, basically, determines the curriculum. The modern teacher implements both small group and individual endeavours in order to provide for individual differences. The traditional teacher stresses large group instruction largely. He/she feels with well prepared lessons, the entire class may be taught at one time. In addition, the modern teacher believes and endorses the following:

- using peer teaching, at intervals, in assisting pupil comprehension of ideas.
- the teacher and peers are both available to assist pupils who have difficulties in learning.
- pupils with teacher guidance being involved in determining standards of conduct in the classroom.
- learners involved in self evaluation as well as teacher observation being utilized.
- the teacher provides for multiple intelligences in the classroom as well as diverse styles of learning.
- a variety of learning opportunities are provided to meet needs of pupils.

- pupils being involved in sequencing their own learnings.

In comparison, traditional teachers stress.

- doing all of the teaching due to their having more maturity and level of education.
- the teacher does most of the assessing in daily work of pupils.
- testing equals teaching in that mandated standardized tests provide feedback in terms of what is necessary to help pupils learn.
- all pupils are treated fairly and alike in that the same curriculum is appropriate for every learner in the classroom.
- leaning heavily upon basal textbooks as learning activities for pupils due to specialists being involved in their writing. Manuals accompanying these texts provide suggestions for related pupil learnings.
- determining sequence or order of provided learning activities in a logical method (Ediger, March 2010).

REFERENCES

Cremin, Lawrence (1977), *Traditions of American Education*. New York: Basic Books.

Dewey, John (1916), *Democracy and Education*. New York: Macmillan Company.

Ediger, Marlow, and D. Bhaskara Rao (2010), *Effective School Curriculum*. New Delhi, India.

Ediger, Marlow (March 2010), *"Constructivism and the Social Studies,"* Edutracks 9 (7), 13-14.

Knight, Edgar (1951), *Education in the United States*. Boston: Ginn and Company.

Leddy, Dana (2010), *"To Understand the Content, Write About It,"* Social Studies and the Young Learner," 23(1), 4-7.

Shepherd, Gene, and William Ragan (1982), *Modern Elementary Curriculum*. Sixth Edition. New York: Holt, Rinehart and Winston.

Tiedt, Iris M. (1982), The Language Arts Handbook. Englewood Cliffs, New Jersey: Prentice Hall, Inc.

Teacher Education and Public Schools

There are a plethora of educational journal articles written on what needs to be emphasized in teacher education. Most of these articles are personal opinions, and if followed would make for continual change, resulting in any lack of continuity or stability. Professors do desire to have their manuscripts published, and in selected universities publish or perish may be the rule. It appears that educators need to take stock of the recommendations and then come up with concrete solutions for *necessary* changes.

News reports may state that the public schools are broken and need repair. This seems to be on a continuum, regardless of changes being made. Too frequently, there is no evidence presented by news reporters on public schools being broken. Public schools have then become a punching bag for frustrations and failures in society. When there is high unemployment, a criticism made is that employers fail to find satisfactory employees for different positions. Schools just have "failed" to educate pupils adequately to fill these vacancies. Businesses fail to take blame for failings in their endeavours. They need to take responsibilities for huge salaries given to CEOs as well as stock options, and bonuses, among other perks. It is indeed ridiculous to give management these benefits which bankrupt companies. To give them $12 million dollar yearly salaries when a company is going bankrupt is unbelievable. People need to become more accountable, service oriented and benevolent. Pensions of workers are lost as well as investment savings wiped out due to selfishness and extreme corruption.

The School Environment

Numerous happenings in the environment hurt pupil achievement in the public schools. Good teaching must always receive primary emphasis; however, there are many other factors affecting learner progress. This is where the community school concept comes into prominence. Poverty is certainly an issue. Children in poor socio-economic situations attending the public schools do poorly compared to those in suburbia. Money buys an abundance of advantages for pupils in the home setting. Homes may then have excellent reading materials for children as well as parents setting a model in encouraging learning through reading. Already at a young age, pupils may emulate this model. Travelling to museums and points of interest, including those abroad, costs money and advantaged homes can provide these benefits to offspring. Additional benefits of having adequate home income include quality clothing, nutritious food, and safe housing. A closely knit community might well remedy societal problems. It takes a sustained group effort to provide safety nets which an economic system has failed to provide.

Too many children face health problems who come from poverty areas. Medical, as well as dental services are either minimal or none existent for these children. Not feeling well definitely hurts achievement. There are reports of children staying home from school to take care of siblings due to low income parents who work at jobs which at the most pay minima) wages, with no health insurance benefits and no future pensions to meet expensive when old age sets in. Budget cuts are, too frequently, emphasized for social services by state and federal governments. This hinders providing for needs of children, in particular.

Public libraries are not open, in many situations, where poverty in the community is in evidence. They could provide valuable services to the poor, as well as others, such as available computer services; too many times poverty/low income homes do not have serviceable computers. Technology is definitely the wave of the future! Libraries, too, need to have suitable reading materials for children as well as adults; they might well provide for avenues of growth and progress for all in reading.

Higher Academic Achievement for Pupils

Schools are asked to do more in advancing learner progress in the school setting. No Child Left Behind (NCLB) is a high stakes test which pupils need to pass in order to be promoted in grades three through eight, and pass on the high school level to receive a diploma. It tests in the areas of reading, mathematics, and science. The scope of the curriculum is too narrow in that social studies, music, art, and physical education achievement are not tested upon. These curriculum areas can provide for needs of pupils to excel and, perhaps, provide for a future vocation of avocation.

There is more to life than academic achievement. Thus, the following facets of growth are, also, highly salient;

- quality attitudes toward life and learning.
- caring for others and feelings of humaneness.
- good human relations.
- co-operation for the common good.
- respect for others.

The above can be woven into any curriculum area and teachers need school time to do this. When preparing for NCLB testing of pupils, teachers feel hurried and pupils seemingly do much memorizing to pass respective NCLB tests.

There is much written about bullying among pupils in school and in society. This is not good for either the perpetrator nor the recipient. Models presented by adults do little for teaching proper social behaviour. The recent elections have shown the ferocity of attacks hurled among candidates—name calling (Communist, Hitlerite, socialist, idiot, among others). Prior to the primary elections of 2008, there were debates to be held among and between candidates of opposite political parties on television. The result was utter chaos, shouting, and acting *crazed*! Nothing had been learned of being civil in society. Mistruths, then, and prior to the elections of 2010, individuals campaigned on the following, in many cases:

- smaller government—but nothing was said about what will be cut in federal spending. A few called for the elimination of social security and medicare.
- reducing taxes. Here, again, there were problems on which to cut. The argument given, many times, was that reducing taxes was a way to stimulate the economy in which the saved tax payer moneys would be used to create jobs and encourage increased consumer spending. However, broad generalities were used in debates.
- balancing the budget. This had its pros and cons in that most felt spending was unnecessary to create jobs.

Specifics are greatly lacking in how to curb spending in a recession and in which areas. Generally, social programmes are the culprit for cutting and encouraging personal wealth becomes the major objective. Areas which need much attention in funding include the following:

- education. NCLB needs full funding, as do numerous other programmes for educating the gifted and talented, renovating and building new school buildings, updating electrical and heating systems, and in general promoting achievement among all classifications of pupils.

- cleaning up polluted scenes involving air, sea and land.
- increased aid to colleges and universities to update facilities and increase learning opportunities.
- more scholarships available to encourage future teachers to enter the profession. Students have mounds of debt after graduation and then enter the area of teaching where salaries are extremely low.

The wealth is there in the United States with its abundant capacity to achieve surplus yields in agriculture on many acres of prime land, for example, but the income from all sources must be used wisely. Spending moneys on useless foreign wars should instead be diverted to domestic programmes which benefit the common good.

CHAPTER 12

Teaching Mathematics and Emotional Intelligence

The mathematics teacher has a plethora of salient responsibilities in the classroom and in society. He/she must plan each lesson and unit appropriately to provide for the needs of each learner. With English Language Learners (ELL) in class, the mathematics teacher must provide for the understanding level of each. Then too, there may be discipline problems which need to be solved, as well as irate parents who must be worked with. With the above named differences, the mathematics teacher needs to be poised and self-disciplined. Too frequently, the emotions take over and rational thought is minimized. The teacher must be in control of their own behaviours so that regret over what was said does not hinder from being an effective mathematics teacher. Emotions can be very helpful in being passionate about teaching mathematics as well as in enjoying teaching as a profession, but they also can provide for hasty, embarrassing statements and actions. Emotional Intelligence (EI) needs to be an inherent part of teaching (Nazareth, 2010).

Teaching Mathematics Effectively

A highly salient part of teaching stresses the importance of mathematics teachers being highly competent of vital subject matter to be imparted to pupils. The teacher then has mastered mathematical facts, concepts, generalizations and skills needed in teaching a given set of learners. He/she must also have diverse methods of teaching available to assist each pupil in context to achieve optimally. This aids in preventing frustration when guiding pupils in diagnosis and remediation of errors in ongoing lessons and units of study. Too frequently, mathematics teachers have vented frustration in working with pupils in these situations. The teacher has then said things which are regretted and learners may lose confidence in the teacher. He/she is human but must remember to be respectful in communications of ideas. A teacher's role, here, is to teach ordered subject matter and be accepting of pupils, not losing one's cool in the midst of an instructional sequence or when discipline problems accrue. With scolding, talking down to, as well as using put downs, both teacher and pupils lose out on quality teaching. What is missed out on by learners must be remedied prior to proceeding with ensuing content. Mathematics is logical and new knowledge builds upon that previously presented. El is emphasized when Schema theory is used in relating connections between the known and the unknown (Ediger and Rao, 2011).

Second, empathy toward others, and pupils in particular, needs to be shown within teaching and learning situations. As a grade school pupil, the writer well remembers when pupils were asked to exchange papers across the aisle with the teacher reading the correct answers to each problem. Each pupil would then mark if an incorrect answer was given with the teacher at the end calling each name and recording in the grade book how many were correct. Pupils who had low scores must have shuddered each day when their name was called for grade recording whereas those with high scores may have liked the procedure. A lack of empathy or feelings for those who were at the bottom of the totem pole. The attitudinal dimension of each pupil must become an inherent part of instruction. Emotional intelligence stresses this as being highly salient.

Third, many teachers/principals lose their positions due to lacking in the ability to work well with others. In the Hutchinson, Kansas News, May 22, 2011 issue, the newspaper headline in bold print indicated the problems faced at an elementary school whereby the teachers had met numerous times in a separate room without the school principal to discuss problems involved when working with the principal of the school. The principal frequently reprimanded teachers in front of their pupils in a rude approach. It is difficult, or impossible, for communication to take place under these circumstances. And yet, the principal is staying on for the next school year in the same position. Without input from the teachers in the elementary school, an administrative decision was made to transfer half of the school's teachers to a different school resulting in eight new teachers. The school board stated that "schools exist for children and they can be assigned where needed." Selected parents and teachers believe strongly they should be consulted prior to transfers taking place. The emotions and feelings of many in this disagreement were entirely omitted. Problems at the work place might result more from negative human relations with strong feelings expressed verbally as compared to a lack of subject matter knowledge and skills in teaching. Paying attention to both, however, is very important; a lack of mathematical knowledge may make for problems in the realm of human relations. Accepting others and working effectively with colleagues is necessary for a school to function well. This is a key component of emotional intelligence (See Goleman, 1998).

Fourth, Self regulation of behaviour stresses the significance of the teacher being able to control his/her own behaviour. In times when things just do not go well, the teacher is able to master personal feelings so that negative comments and statements do not get in the way of doing things well. All are faced at times with frustrations where goals, major and minor, are not attained. The teacher needs to focus upon the successes experienced whereby a good self-concept is developed. Teachers must be aware of their feelings of self-confidence, emotions, as well as the ability to regulate one's own behaviour. Being able to do this, in degrees, facilitates working with pupils and other teachers in the mathematics curriculum. El advocates that being aware of the feelings of the self will assist in working more effectively with pupils and other teachers. There are teachers who lack El when working with parents, as in parent/teacher conferences, especially in self-regulation. When a parent is critical of the teacher in providing help when needed in mathematics, the teacher may then become defensive and show signs of mistrust; rather, the teacher must face each situation honestly and openly with the intent of growth and achievement as a mathematics instructor. Reflecting upon past experiences and modifying behaviour is a must! Learning then accrues in becoming increasingly professional (See Bandura, 1997).

Fifth, empathy for the feelings of others is imperative for teachers. Pupils, parents, among others in a school district, have feelings about happenings, events, and the environment. It would be good if major decisions could be made objectively or in a scientific manner, but this is not possible in many cases. With subjectivity involved, feelings accrue and are then in evidence. With curbs being placed on school spending due to limited finances available, there is a lack of agreement on which cuts and how they should be made on the following:

- teachers and support personnel positions and salaries.
- the number of school administrators in a district.

- textbooks, paper for printers and art work, equipment, as well as computer additions and replacements.
- pupils/parents paying for participation in selected athletic and musical endeavours.
- redoing bus routes for economic reasons.
- eliminating/reducing art and music instruction in the curriculum.

Emotions are very strong on the national level as to cuts in spending to be made in the following budgetary items:

- social security, medicare, and Medicaid.
- defense, military operations, and security.
- infrastructure including highways (interstate and non-interstate), bridges, prisons, police and fire protection.

It takes much effort within the framework of emotional intelligence to harmonize efforts in working toward solutions. On the national level in Congress, it certainly has been difficult to solve these major problems. Feelings of empathy have been at an almost zero level. EI needs stress not only in the school setting and in the mathematics curriculum but also in the societal arena (See Goleman, 1995).

Sixth, social skills are very important when emphasizing emotional intelligence. Interpersonal skills are highly salient in collaborative endeavours in mathematics. Pupils may truly learn much when working co-operatively to solve mathematical problems. Ideas then "bounce" off the minds of participants and circulate within the small group endeavour. Learning becomes a social task with involved others. Problem solving involves a dilemma situation whereby the problem must be clearly defined and delimited, related information sought to problem solve, resulting in an hypothesis, the hypothesis is to be tested through discussion and other practical means. If the hypothesis holds up under scrutiny, it is upheld, but if not, additional information needs to be sought in answer to the problem. There are a plethora of examples pertaining to the kinds and types of problems which arise in mathematics:

- finding the area in square units of a carpet to be installed in the classroom.
- solving an algebraic expression with one unknown.
- factoring and finding the least common denominator or greatest common factor.

When collaborative endeavours are important in the classroom, the following standards need adherence:

- all need to participate in the ongoing experience with no one dominating the activity.
- ideas must be respected and participants accepted.
- content must be presented clearly with active participation.
- ideas need to circulate within the committee.
- pupils need to stay on task (Ediger and Rao, 2000).

Weaknesses in collaborative work must be diagnosed and remedied. This includes hostility of members. EI is salient here. Those who shirk must be involved and do their fair share of the work. Otherwise, these individuals are not achieving objectives. Accepting of other's ideas in a discussion is important with modifications made as needed within the group. If digression occurs within the problem solving activity, pupils must understand this wastes time in securing an answer to the problem. Ideas that do not circulate within the committee may mean that individuals are left out of small group work. Accepting the feelings of others is salient in small group work.

REFERENCES

Bandura, Albert (1997), *Self Efficacy: The Exercise of Control*. New York: Freeman.

Ediger, Marlow, and D. Bhaskara Rao (2011). *Readings on the Teaching of Mathematics*. New Delhi, India; Discovery Publishing House.

Ediger, Marlow, and D. Bhaskara Rao (2000), *Teaching Mathematics Successfully.* New Delhi, India; Discovery Publishing House.

Goleman, Daniel (1998), *Working with Emotional Intelligence.* New York: Bantam Books.

Goleman, Daniel (1995), *Emotional Intelligence*. New York; Bantam Books.

Nazareth, Bruno (2010), *Effect of Emotional Intelligence and Self Efficacy* of B. Ed. Trainees on their Academic Achievement. Ph.D, thesis Appraised by the writer (Marlow Ediger) for Alagappa University, Kodaikal, India.

CHAPTER 13

Improving Achievement in Mathematics

How might pupil achievement in mathematics be improved? This manuscript will pertain to upping progress by incorporating major psychological principles. Pupils may be turned off in math lessons due to routine procedures, resulting in feelings of boredom. Instead, there is much the teacher may do to motivate learning.

Maximizing Achievement

The mathematics teacher might well reduce feelings of boredom by using a variety of activities. Thus, the teacher may utilize the concrete phase with objects and items; the semi-concrete with illustrations, transparencies, life-like problems coming from learners, the hand held calculator, the computer and internet; and the abstract such as word problems, functional worksheets and the basal textbook. Varying the types of activities for pupils on their individual development level might make for stimulating experiences, especially if designed to obtain personal interests. Active involvement of learners is a must in ongoing lessons and units of study (Ediger, 2007).

Second, pupils may be assisted in achieving challenging goals through bridging; thus the teacher helps pupils overcome the gap between present and a higher desired level of attainment. The mathematics teacher may then sequence questions so that the pupil might attain the ensuing objective. The ordered responses of the learner aid in attaining the new objective of instruction. Bridging is a very valuable concept for teachers to emphasize in teaching and learning situations. Pupils need to feel challenge and yet experience success in teaching and learning situations. The teacher with mathematical knowledge and skills is, especially, trained and educated to assist each category of learner be it the gifted/talented, the average achievers, English Language Learners (ELL), the special needs child, and/or pupils from lower income level homes to attain as optimally as possible (See the National Council Teachers of Mathematics, 1989).

Third, pupils need to believe in themselves to become efficacious learners. Here, pupils have confidence and a good self-concept to develop achieve, and grow in knowledge, skills, and attitudes. The quality mathematics teacher, too, needs to possess efficacy in that he/she is confident in teaching any category of learner to attain optimally. Efficacy comes from developing mathematical competency in subject matter, methods of instruction, and the emotional (attitudinal dimension) domain. There are educators who advocate Emotional Intelligence (EI) to be highly salient in that good attitudes toward mathematics instruction aids in becoming competent in the subject matter of mathematics as well as its related teaching skills (See Nolan, 2003).

Fourth, metacognition skills assists the learner to reflect upon what has been learned and what is left to learn. Through reflection, the pupil not only rehearses previous content acquired, but also assesses where gaps and misunderstandings have occurred. Diagnosis and remediation then become salient since that which is not meaningful may become so. The teacher needs to model the correct response or reasoning used to solve a word problem. Metacognition not only aids pupils to rehearse and retain mathematical learnings but also use reason to correct errors.

Fifth, it is important to identify learning styles of pupils to ascertain which procedure is most beneficial for learners. Selected pupils do best in large group instruction where a multiplicity of activities capture pupil's attention. Others prefer small group endeavours whereby collaboration is involved among participants. Each may challenge others in the small group so all achieve well. Still others, prefer individual endeavours whereby the learner prefers to work by the self. Adequate provisions must be made for every pupil and no one should fall through the cracks. Time on task is valuable with much being expected from learners within the allotted time (Ediger, 2010).

Sixth, the math curriculum needs continual updating with the latest in technology to facilitate the learning process. Technology involving computer use might well guide learners to achieve more optimally. Technology assists pupils to attain relevant content and skills needed in the 21st century and to compete favourably with other nations in the world, such as Finland and Singapore. Computer programmes must emphasize problem solving, reasoning, diagnosis and remediation, as well as simulations, among others, which motivate pupil learning to attain objectives. School supervisors must provide inservice education to guide teachers in making the fullest use of technology in curriculum improvement. Mathematics teachers need to develop confidence in using technology to provide for each category of learner in securing knowledge, skills, and quality attitudes.

Seventh, mathematics teachers need continual encouragement to upgrade professional instruction. The following approaches are highly recommended:

- working toward an advanced degree at an approved college/university.

- doing an independent study on an area of weakness in teaching mathematics to fill the void in strengthening teaching and learning.
- taking online course work in mathematics subject matter and procedures of instruction.
- managing the classroom effectively to maximum mathematics.
- achievement as well as improve the attitudinal dimension.
- study innovative programmes such as cognitive mapping strategies with plans, if the study so warrants, to implement salient concepts (see, Vadivu, 2010).

REFERENCES

Ediger, Marlow (2007), *"Learning Activities in the Curriculum,"* College Student Journal, 41 (4), 967-969.

Ediger, Marlow (2010), *"Collaboration in Improving the Mathematics Curriculum,"* Montana Mathematics," March, pp 13-14.

The National Council Teachers of Mathematics (1989), *Curriculum and Evaluation Standards for School Mathematics.* Reston, Virginia: NCTM.

Nolan, Jennifer (2003), *"Multiple Intelligences in the Classroom/ Education",* 124(1), 115-119.

Vadivu, P. Pandia (2010), *Effect of Metacognitive Strategies on Concept Mapping in Learning in Biology Education.* Kodaikanal, India: Mother Teresa Women's University. Ph.D. Thesis evaluated by the writer Marlow Ediger.

Mathematics and Psychology of Learning

Teachers of mathematics need to have a strong background of course in work and pedagogy, as well as inservice educational opportunities in teaching mathematics. In addition, they must keep abreast of recommended methods of instruction through reading of journal information pertaining to instructional practices.

Pupils deserve quality instruction in order to achieve as optimally as possible. Knowledge and skills secured need to be useful in school and in the community. Trivia and useless information need to be culled to make room for the relevant and functional subject matter. The psychology of learning can do much to assist mathematics teachers in helping pupils to attain objectives of instruction.

Psychology of Teaching Mathematics

Mathematics teachers need to be highly knowledgeable about the psychology of learning and how its use might well facilitate pupil learning. First of all, it behooves teachers to facilitate learners in ongoing activities to be actively involved in achieving. Passive, uninvolved pupils will hardly achieve worthwhile objectives. Thus, the teacher must develop learner interest in the ensuing mathematical experiences. Materials of instruction need to be as concrete as possible on the pupil's developmental level. Thus, for example, on the early primary grade levels, pupils might use wooden blocks in counting in one to one correspondence. As the child points to each block in counting and orally says the cardinal number, meaning is attached to an ongoing activity. For older pupils, such as on the senior high school level, the teacher assists pupils in using what has been learned in a concrete life-like situation. There is a purpose then in learning which is functional in school and in society.

Learnings which are relevant and useful aid pupils in becoming involved in achievement. What is understood and has meaning increases opportunities for pupils to actively participate in ensuing lesson and unit experiences. Next, pupils need to have ample experiences in practicing what has been acquired. This may be enhanced through meta-cognition strategies. Here, the mathematics teacher assists pupils to reflect and think about previous learnings. When reflecting in answer to vital questions, the pupil makes use of salient facts, concepts, and generalizations. He/she also reveals what is not meaningful; gaps in learning need to be filled with sequential information. What is lacking in sequence may make for difficulties later on when increasingly more complex subject matter is being learned. Previous learnings provide building blocks for ensuing subject matter. Retention of knowledge and skills is important for establishing meaning and understanding as well as making it possible to use these learnings in achieving higher levels of cognition. Meta-cognition skills in reflective thinking then are useful presently as well as in future endeavours such as at a work place.

Scaffolding needs equate stress in the mathematics curriculum. Here, the pupil is at a certain level, for example, in multiplying fractions with unlike denominators and with scaffolding might attain at a more complex level in multiplying mixed numbers. The knowledgeable teacher then is competent to assist learners in achieving the new objective, but this is possible with appropriate assistance by utilizing a variety of materials of instruction. Mandated testing emphasizes demonstrated pupil achievement on tests; scaffolding might very well be a psychological principle to be used in upping learner progress in measuring progress, providing that meaning is attached to acquired mathematical subject matter.

Adhering to styles of learning has assisted many pupils to do well in the curriculum. Thus, there are pupils who achieve more optimally in collaborative endeavours with each pupil in the committee contributing to their success. Pupils then co-operate as well as challenge each other to achieve, grow, and develop in mathematics. The sharing of ideas provides a framework for each to use his/her talents for the good of the group in mathematical problem solving experiences and at the same time emphasize social attainment within the committee. In comparison to collective endeavours, selected pupils attain more optimally in working by the self. These learners achieve best when personally engaged in the ongoing objective and task. There, no doubt, needs to be opportunities for both collective and individual endeavours in mathematics. Why? In the community, individuals do math both ways since the citizen solves personal mathematics problems, and also works collectively at the work place. A rational balance between the two must exist in the curriculum since individual and collective needs are in evidence in school and in society.

Another salient factor in the psychology of learning is that evaluation should provide feedback from pupils to the teacher for ensuing learning opportunities. Appraisal may well be continuous with the use of teacher observation. Here, the teacher may assist a pupil as soon as possible when an error has been made such as in carrying in addition or multiplication. The teacher may then inductively/deductively help a pupil to engage in more complex learnings sequentially. The teacher must be highly capable of diagnosis and remediation in ongoing lessons and units of study. It is best to have a developmental programme of instruction for all pupils, but this is not possible when pupils, individually or collectively, reveal that which needs more emphasis in teaching. Formative evaluation is done along the way when a mathematical unit is being taught; here, the teacher assesses pupil achievement at regular intervals through valid and reliable tests. The test results give information to the teacher on success in teaching as well as what learners need more help in such as reducing fractions to lowest terms or determining the least common multiple. The items missed by pupils then provide guidance to the mathematics teacher for ensuing teaching and learning situations. Clarification of remedial objectives assist the teacher to provide meaningful experiences for teachers. Pupils need to perceive the purpose of each sequential activity for remediation. This may be stated clearly by the teacher when aiding pupils to see errors made on the formative test; this should motivate pupils to achieve ordered progress.

In addition to formative evaluation, summation assessment should also be in the offing. Thus, at the end of a unit of study, the teacher notices what needs to be changed in terms of objectives, learning opportunities, as well as appraisal procedures for the next time the mathematics unit is taught. Summative evaluation then stresses end of the unit appraisal to ascertain what should possibly be modified to make for greater success in ensuing teaching and learning situations.

Conclusion

Mathematics teachers need to stay abreast of the latest psychological recommendations in order to provide more adequately for each pupil in the classroom. Providing learning opportunities which are meaningful, purposeful, and engage learner interests is vital. Meta-cognition skills are salient in that the learner reviews previous learnings to ascertain what was not understood and then what to do to close these gaps. Scaffolding aids pupils to reach new heights in learning with sequential content to realize the more complex ideas in mathematics. Relevant subject matter increases the chances of pupils using previously encountered mathematical facts, concepts, and generalizations. Styles of learning, too, need ample teacher attention whether it be in collaborate or individual endeavours. Formative and summative evaluation in unit teaching assist the teacher to plan more effectively for ongoing as well as end of unit endeavours.

CHAPTER 15

Mathematics for All Pupils

Mathematics has always been considered as a basic in the curriculum. The familiar concept of the three r's reading, writing, and (a)rithmetic indicates its historical salience. With No Child Left Behind law passed in 2002, it is as essential as ever. This law emphasized testing of pupils in grades three through eight for promotional purposes, in mathematics, reading, and science. Then too, in society, individuals use mathematics in every day transactions. It is practical, useful, and relevant for all pupils to be successful achievers in this academic area A mathematics curriculum needs development which encourages, motivates, and challenges learners to achieve, grow, and accomplish as much as individual abilities and interests provide (Ediger, 2010).

The Psychology of Learning and Mathematics teachers must observe pupils carefully to notice pupil problems which arise in learning. Too frequently, teachers attempt to cover much content in a short period of time without paying attention to learners having mastered what is taught. Psychologist David Ausubel (1978) stated that the most import factor in teaching is to start where pupils are presently in achievement. Thus, if pupils are studying a unit on addition of fractions, the teacher must be certain that learners understand why one-fourth plus one-fourth equals one half. This can be shown meaningfully with one-fourth of a circle being placed adjacent to another congruent one-fourth. Concrete and semi-concrete materials must be inherent to make learnings understandable in teaching. The abstract numerals need to be written next to the two congruent fourths which equal one half. Ensuing subject matter may then be taught in relating the new with that learned previously. The sequence must be as seamless as possible.

If the sequence lacks proper order, pupils may be lost in achieving the new objective. The mathematics teacher must pay careful attention to ordering experiences properly for pupils. When learners understand the meaning of addition of proper fractions, a question may arise by a pupil on names to be applied to fractions such as numerator and denominator. Sequence then resides within involved pupils. These terms should be printed neatly on the word wall for pupil reference and also for their discussion interests when congregating here. Many pupils review and elaborate on meanings when seeing and discussing vocabulary terms on the word wall. Learners also sequence subject matter when, for example, they ask questions about other names for the above two fourths such as three sixths, four eights, among others, each being shown in meaning with three sixths of a circle being placed on one half (Ediger and Rao, 2002). Visual cues are salient in teaching fractions such as circles, squares, software projections on a white board, and slides projections.

Verbal cues should promote effectives of visuals. They should be clear with proper voice inflections to secure learner attention. Stressing selected words more so than others helps pupils to focus upon these salient vocabulary terms, such as proper and improper fractions. The teacher's voice with appropriate prosody can be a very effective means of obtaining pupil attention. Gesture clues should be used to further pupil attentiveness. Here, a logical sequence may be initiated when teacher judgement is used in pointing to the word wall to reinforce a concept and its definition, such as equivalent fractions. Included facial expressions such as a nod of approval or a smile when learners respond correctly is included in non-verbal communication (See Kindervater, 2010).

Levels of Thinking in Mathematics

Pupils need to use different levels of thinking or cognition in ongoing units of study. *Recalling of information* is salient since this provides building blocks for higher cognitive levels. After meaning has been attached, pupils may need to recall how to reduce a fraction to lowest terms. Clearly stating how this operation is performed is necessary to reveal mastery.

The next level of cognition indicates understanding of what was recalled. Thus, for instance, pupils need to demonstrate how a fraction is reduced to lowest terms. What are the understandings needed in reducing fractions? Sequentially the pupil reveals understanding in the order of performing this operation.

Elaborating indicates a more complex level of cognition. Pupils may be challenged to change a mixed number to an improper fraction and describe its meaning. Scaffolding may occur here whereby the teacher may assist by using manipulative materials. This involves the teacher logically helping learners to change a mixed number to an improper fraction. With elaboration, pupils attain content in greater depth with increased understanding. Elaboration should not be hurried since "covering ground" is not the goal in teaching mathematics, but assisting learners to become ready for sequential achievement is salient. Going from the known to the unknown is sacrosanct. Teachers must assist pupils to go from what is known to the ensuing unknown in teaching and learning situations. Elaboration should assist in achieving this objective with learners raising questions to work toward clarification. Too frequently, pupils have memorized subject matter for a test, but meaning has been lacking; indepth learning should help pupils to attach understanding to loose ends of the mathematics curriculum (See Nolan, 2003).

Metacognition guides pupils to reflect upon previous learnings. Learners need assistance in thinking about what they know and what they do not understand. This could be modeled verbally by the teacher in providing a clear model for pupils. With careful attention to each step of learning, pupils individually may use this model in and for metacognition. Metacognition can help pupils to retain knowledge and skills. It does involve rehearsing previously acquired subject matter as well as having a diagnostic purpose. The diagnosis stresses viewing problematic situations in pupil learning with remedies in the offing. It is best to have a developmental mathematics curriculum whereby seamlessly pupil accomplish, develop and grow, but at times and with reflection, diagnosis reveals what needs additional attention in teaching. For example, in the division of fractions, pupils and the teacher might discover that the former does not understand the reasons for inverting the divisor and multiply. The author remembers in grade school when he was taught to divide fractions by simply "turning the divisor upside down" and then doing the familiar which is multiplying. He does not recall any reasons given for doing this. It does make rote learning a concept easier, but it does not provide for meaning in terms of building blocks for sequential achievement. Each learning acquired assists in attaining the more complex, ordered mathematical ideas (Ediger, 2007).

Critical thinking should also be a major objective in mathematics. Here, the pupil learns to separate the relevant from the irrelevant. For example, in doing a word problem, there might be information that is not needed (extraneous content) in solving the problem. Also, the learner might not be following the sequence necessary in solving the problem. One item on a test observed by the author when supervising student teachers dealing with fractions pertained to pupils arranging four fractions from the largest to smallest in value: 2/3 3/4 5/7 6/7. Here, the test item deals with critical thinking in being able to discern the number of parts an object is divided into (the denominator) as compared to the parts being considered (the numerator) as in two of three parts being considered in the fraction 2/3. Critical thinking, here, involves analyzing and making comparisons in arriving which order to show the arranged fractions from largest to smallest (See Scafidi and Bui, 2010).

Creative thinking is also salient as a mental process. The pupil here reveals novel, unique ideas. Originality is a key concept. A pupil might be encouraged in creative endeavours in the following:

- arriving at a different solution in solving a word problem.
- making a collage from different colours of construction paper.
- using cut-out geometrical figures consisting of circles. squares, triangles, among others. Pupils need to identify each geometrical shape in doing the art project.
- writing word problems for other pupils to solve.
- dictating a story by young children for the teacher or aid to record. Older learners may do their own writing in long hand or with word processor use.
- brainstorming how any one fraction being studied may be useful in everyday life.

The mathematics teacher must plan carefully to provide for individual differences. In most classrooms, there are English Language Learners (ELL), handicapped learners, and diverse minority groups which definitely should also have the best in mathematics teaching and learning situations.

They need attainable, challenging objectives, varied learning opportunities which provide for different intelligences, as well as activities that make adequate provision for different styles of learning. A cookie cutter approach where one size fits all is not approbate in a modern mathematics curriculum. Evaluation of achievement needs to be valid and reliable. Optimal achievement is desired from each category of pupils. Diverse appraisal need to be used to assess learner progress including portfolios, teacher written and standardized tests, teacher observation, pupil and teach self evaluation, rating scales, discussions, rubrics, and checklists, among others. Feedback from pupil evaluation results should inform instruction, including the need for higher levels of cognition (See, National Council Teachers of Mathematics, 1989).

In ongoing mathematical units of study, the teacher may find it difficult to ascertain where *clarification* is needed to assist learners in attaching meaning to a concept or generalization. Pupils need encouragement to raise questions pertaining to what lacks meaning and understanding. Pupils may feel uncomfortable in asking for assistance. To minimize/ alleviate these feelings, the mathematics teacher may do the following:

- develop a classroom environment which is relaxing and conducive to learning.
- ask questions in an atmosphere of trust which pinpoint problems in pupil's understanding a specific process or particular knowledge.
- encourage self-evaluation on the part of pupils including diagnosis and remediation.
- have a support system whereby pupils assist each other to achieve.
- sequence learnings which bridge the gap for pupils between the known and the unknown.
- attain pupil efficacy whereby pupils feel confident in ensuing learning opportunities (See Palvanivassan, 2006).

Additional Factors in Teaching

With adequate inservice education and recognition given for quality teaching, the mathematics teacher might well gain self-confidence in ongoing units of study. A quality self-concept is needed for teachers to become increasingly effective in teaching all categories of learners. Efficacious teachers know how to provide for individual differences in assisting each pupil to achieve more optimally.

To select what pupils are to achieve, the mathematics teacher must be well versed in mathematical content and methods of teaching. Key, structural ideas need to be acquired by pupils; trivia must be avoided. Inservice education should involve not only teachers and school administrators but also professors from nearby universities who specialize in mathematics education. Major generalizations might then be identified for pupil acquisition. Inservice education should also focus upon procedures and processes to be used by pupils in learning such as using inquiry methods, project methods, problem solving, rational thinking, a learning by doing approach, as well as constructivism as a psychology of learning. Rote learning is to be discouraged unless meaning is stressed therein. For quality sequence to occur, the pupil needs to build on previous learnings and this emphasizes learners understanding what is taught and learned.

REFERENCES

Ausubel David (1978), *Educational Psychology: A Cognitive View*. New York: Holt, Rinehart and Winston.

Ediger, Marlow (2010), *"Collaboration in Improving the Mathematics Curriculum,"* Montana Mathematics, March, pp 13-14, Published by the Montana Council Teachers of Mathematics.

Ediger, Marlow, and D. Bhaskara Rao (2002), *Teaching Mathematics Successfully*. New Delhi, India: Discovery Publishing House.

Ediger, Marlow (2007) *"Learning Activities in the Curriculum,"* College Student Journal, 41 (4), 967-969.

Kindervater, Terry (2010), *"Family Literacy,"* The Reading Teacher, 63(7), 610-613.

National Council Teachers of Mathematics (1989), *Curriculum and Evaluation Standards for School Mathematics.* Reston, Virginia: NCTM.

Nolan, Jennifer L, (2003), *"Multiple Intelligences in the Classroom,"* Education, 124(1), 115-119.

Palvanivassan, M. (2006), *Analysis of Errors Committed by Higher Secondary Students in Calculus.* Ph,D.thesis evaluated by the writer (Ediger) for the University of Madras, Chennai, India.

Scafidi, Tony, and Khanh Bui (2010), *"Gender Similarities in Math Performance from Middle School Through High School,"* Journal of Instructional Psychology, 37 (3), 252-255.

Diagnosis and Remediation in Mathematics Curriculum

The teacher must have a quality background of subject matter content in mathematics, not only for teaching but also for viewing pupil errors which need correction. In each mathematical unit of study, the teacher must choose important content for instruction, not trivia. Each pupil needs to perceive interest, purpose, and meaning in mathematics. It would indeed be excellent if the teacher, inductively/deductively, would continually sequences learnings appropriately. Even then, there are pupils who do not connect with the ongoing lesson. Thus, the teacher must be a good diagnostician and remediator of gaps in learning which learners possess (Ediger, 1997).

Assisting Pupils in Learning

Which are selected common errors pupils reveal in ongoing mathematical units of study? These need to be studied by each teacher in the classroom. Collectively, teachers should also meet to discuss the concepts of diagnosis and remediation of pupil mistakes. Improving the curriculum involves teachers working together with effective human relations involved.

The relations need to involve respecting each other's ideas in an atmosphere of trust. Building on subject matter discussed, teachers might well develop a repertoire of knowledge and skills in teaching mathematics (See National Council Teachers of Mathematics, 1989). Pupils, too, need to experience an atmosphere of acceptance and belonging. It becomes more profitable then for teachers and pupils to analyze difficulties in mathematics and stress synthesis. One major problem faced by pupils is the lack of computational skills. With addition and subtraction of whole numbers, fractions, and decimals, there are numerous specifics to view. Pupils too often have memorized addition facts, for example, without understanding and attaching meaning. These are foundational learnings and pupils will later in sequence deal with increased complexity of mathematical operations. Meaningful subject matter must always be in the offing. Computational errors must be diagnosed as soon as possible and with teacher observation used to evaluate progress so that learners do not practice what is incorrect (See Kennedy and Tipps, 1991).

Second, pupils need to use reason properly when pursuing ongoing learnings. For instance, a pupil might believe that 3/8 is larger in value than 3/4 until a circle is divided into eight parts and three of these are considered whereas the second fraction, the circle is divided into four parts and three of these are being considered. Here, the pupil can see which is larger of the two fractions and use reason in ordered learnings. Being able to think through a problematic situation, most pupils are able to come up with answers to questions (Ediger and Rao, 2000).

Third, pupils need to develop a systematic approach in problem solving. Too frequently, pupils may jump around hastily from one procedure to another without additional means of solving a problem. When solving word problems, pupils fail to ask questions such as:

- what is wanted in a final answer?

- which essential information is needed sequentially to problem solve?
- is there information presented which is not needed in arriving at a solution?
- what questions do I need to ask the teacher to clarify what is not understood?
- do I know the appropriate operation on involved numbers to solve the problem (Ediger, 2007).

When giving assistance to pupils, the mathematics teacher may use inquiry methods whereby the teacher provides clues such as verbal, gestural, pictorial, audio, and concrete materials to guide pupil progress.

Fourth, pupils make computational errors which need diagnosis. This might well mean that basic addition, subtraction, multiplication, and division facts have not been mastered, or haste and sloppy performance are inherent. It does save time and effort if essential leanings have been mastered when pursuing new learnings. Diagnosis would involve if the same errors are made again and again by a pupil, and yet these are not beyond the developmental level of the learner. By calling specific kinds of errors to a pupils attention, he/she should perceive purpose with remediation in ongoing lessons and units of study (Scafadi and Bui, 2001).

Fifth, lacking fluency in reading causes difficulties in doing word problems. Mathematics instruction should not become a reading course. However, it is difficult to separate reading skills from the academic discipline of mathematics. Thus, it becomes imperative for the teacher to identify the kinds of errors made by a pupil when reading math word problems. Calling pupils attention to the importance of using context clues may help many pupils. A difficulty in using phonics such as the initial consonant of a word needs remediation and provides the learner with an approach in attacking unknown words. Other phonic elements may be stressed in teaching as needed to help pupils in developing word attack skills. The mathematics teacher needs to be a teacher of reading in order to assist learners to identify words fluently while reading to solve mathematical problems. Comprehension of subject matter is the ultimate goal (Ediger, 2010).

Sixth, vocabulary development is salient since selected learners do not understand concepts inherent in ongoing lessons and units of study. These words may come from reading word problems and also those utilized in discussions. Addends, minuend, subtrahend, factoring, inverting, among others, need elaboration and then placed on a classroom word wall. The math teacher may refer pupils to these words as needed. The writer when supervising university student teachers noticed how studious learners were when viewing these words and discussing them at break time. Pupils do have an inward desire to learn.

Seventh, selected pupils lack an adequate attention span to benefit from the ensuing learning opportunities in mathematics. If the activities are too complex, the mathematics teacher may remedy the situation by adjusting teaching and learning situations to the present achievement level of the learner. Then too, the explanations given may be simplified by using terminology which pupils understand. Materials of instruction used might be more concrete in nature. Thus, objects may be used together with the abstract words and concepts in providing for meaningful instruction. The pace of experiences provided should harmonize with what pupils can master in time. The point being that math teachers need to observe pupils at work and diagnose what needs improvement. Remediation then is based upon observations made on a daily basis. Test results, too, may provide excellent feedback on where pupils fail in attaching meaning in the mathematics curriculum. These situations might well make for turning off and loosing interest in achieving. Computers and technology have advanced to provide for selected excellent programmes to secure and maintain pupils interest in the curriculum (Martinez, 2010).

Eighth, pupils fail to understand and use structural ideas in mathematics. Attaching meaning to and utilizing a structure of knowledge assists the pupil in developing proficiency in doing math. Thus, for example, the commutative and associative properties of addition and multiplication provide learners a method of viewing computation and their possibilities in performing operations on number. Also, patterns involved in working with number might well fascinate and interest pupils in mathematics.

Conclusion

By diagnosing and remedying pupil progress in mathematics, learners might find interest and purpose in ongoing lessons and units of study. The curriculum then is adjusted to their present achievement levels. Being frustrated and having a feeling of being lost in an activity, pupils may experience change with motivation and interest in learning and achieving objectives of instruction.

REFERENCES

Ediger, Marlow (1997), *Teaching Mathematics in the Elementary School.* Kirksville, Missouri: Simpson Publishing Company.

Ediger, Marlow (2007), *Learning Activities in the Curriculum*, College Student Journal, 41 (4), 967-969.

Ediger, Marlow, and D. Bhaskara Rao (2000), *Teaching Mathematics Successfully.* New Delhi, India: Discovery Publishing House.

Ediger, Marlow (2010), *Enjoyment in the Mathematics Curriculum*, Montana Mathematics, 43 (3), 12-15.

Kennedy, Leonard, and Steve Tipps (1991), *Guiding Children's Learning of Mathematics.* Belmont, California: Wadsworth Publishing company.

National Council Teachers of Mathematics (1989), *Curriculum and Evaluation Standards for School Mathematics.* Reston, Virginia: NCTM.

Scafadi, Tony and Khanh Bui (2010), *Gender Similarities in Math Performance from Middle School Through High School,* Journal of Instructional Psychology, 37 (3), 262-255.

Martinez, Monica (2010), *"Teacher Education Can't Ignore Technology,"* Phi Delta Kappan, 92 (2), 74-75.

CHAPTER 17

Pointers in Teaching Science

There are selected criteria which need to be followed in teaching ongoing lessons and units of study in science. By following each criterion, pupils optimize achievement in the science curriculum. Achieving objectives in science teaching, pupils may progress sequentially in a carefully designed programme. Which criteria should science teachers follow in teaching/learning situations?

Guidelines in the Teaching of Science

Teachers need to have high expectations from instruction and pupil learning. Too frequently, teachers expect minimal achievement from selected learners. Instead, the science teacher must expect optimal progress from each pupil. With carefully chosen learning opportunities, pupils feel challenged to grow and accomplish. These activities need to engage pupils, are interesting and possess perceived purpose. All seem to be actively involved if the activities attract attention. This is the way it should be in teaching science. When supervising university student teachers with co-operating teacher guidance, the writer observed in one class where pupils were inattentive in a science unit on "The Changing Surface of the Earth." Much lecture was used in teaching and pupils appeared lethargic, and yet the content might have been very engaging for pupils. Pupils, for example, tend to be fascinated with volcanic eruptions, glaciers, soil/wind erosion, floods, hurricanes/tornados, among other destructive forces. Models, power point, illustrations, videos, print sources, science experiments and demonstrations, as well as excursions (erosion of soil might well be observed on the school grounds), provide relevant materials of instruction for learners to attain carefully chosen objectives. There are excellent reading materials, for instance, pertaining to natural disasters in current events newspapers, internet sources, as well as the basal science textbook. High expectations, within reason, as well as interesting materials and discussions can certainly engage pupil in ongoing lessons and units of study. Scaffolding may be utilized by the science teacher to assist pupils in achieving more complex learnings (Ediger and Rao, 2010).

Purpose in learning is very significant in aiding learner progress. If pupils do not see relevance in subject matter being studied, they will tend to possess low energy levels for achievement. There are numerous approaches then which may be used to guide pupils to notice how subject matter content might be utilized. Selected pupils have read how a tornado completely wiped out a small town or did heavy damage in larger cities. For example, Greensburg, Kansas, a small city and now almost completely rebuilt, was totally destroyed by a tornado in 2007, except for a very few structures. A well built, brick grade school was entirely demolished to show tornado strength in an aftermath. The President of the United States made several visits to this small city. There are other tornados such as hurricane Katrina in New Orleans which pupils have heard/read about which were equally powerful. Pupils need to be actively engaged in ongoing learning opportunities in current events involving science news (Ediger, 2010).

Meaningful experiences need to be in the offing for pupils in science. These must be personalized which assist to ensure learner success. Thus, for example to lecture/explain to pupils that air has weight and takes up space, learners may be engaged in putting a tissue paper in an inverted tumbler and press it straight down into the water filled aquarium. Prior to doing this experiment, learners need to hypothesize as to what will happen to the tissue. These may be printed on the board for all to see clearly. Pupils need to understand that hypotheses are subject to testing. The experiment needs to be performed where all can clearly notice a dry tissue inside the tumbler. Meaning is attached to an important science concept. Additional experiments may be performed to confirm the correct hypothesis. Understanding of subject matter is salient; memorization, alone, is inadequate. Ensuing meaningful subject matter will be based upon what is clearly understood in the present learning opportunities. Success in meaningful achievement is significant for all in the school/classroom setting (See National Research Council, 1996).

Metacognitive strategies should be used so that pupils recognize what has/has not be acquired. Thus, the pupil is assisted to reflect upon what was learned in order to reinforce and retain relevant concepts and generalizations. Then too, the pupil will realize gaps in learning. These gaps need to be alleviated through additional sequential learning opportunities. They may also be filled through scaffolding. Here, the teacher may deductively present brief meaningful explanations which the pupil can utilize in understanding ensuing knowledge and skills. Scaffolding may also fill gaps through inductive experiences whereby the science teacher raises ordered questions which assist the learner to arrive successfully in understanding the new content (See Bybee, 1997).

Problem solving and inquiry learning are at the heart of teaching and learning situations in science. Pupils, individually or collectively, with teacher guidance raise purposeful questions which require effort and perseverance in their solving. The questions are meaningful since the pupil has an inward desire to achieve necessary answers. Quite frequently, experimentation provides needed information. Depending upon the maturation level of learners, a question, for example, may arise pertaining to what plants need in order to grow. Thus, two potted bean plants containing equivalent stock and soil with the same appropriate moisture, may be set on a window ledge. Pupils then may hypothesize what happens when a paper sack is placed over one plant. Careful observation is necessary with not jumping to hasty conclusions pertaining to the results. Testing for one variable may also involve differences in moisture provided, differences in the type of soil, and differences in temperature readings for one potted plant as compared to the other. Methods of science may be stressed here with testing one variable, as well as developing/revising an hypothesis, if necessary. New problems are identified along the way as an experiment progresses (See Martinez, 2010).

Problem solving is a useful skill in that individuals rather continuously identify major/minor problems which need solutions. Then too, problem solving is useful in society as well as in school.

Pupils need to feel confident in problem solving and inquiry methods as approaches in securing information. Self efficacy must then being an ongoing objective in science. The efficacious science teacher possesses the following:

- feels challenge in teaching and learning situations.
- believes he/she is capable of teaching any set of learners regardless of socio-economic levels or ethnicity.
- enjoys teaching science due to being able to motivate learning in science.

- reads science subject matter from a variety of reliable reference sources including the internet. Ideas gleaned are used to improve the science curriculum.
- does science experiments and demonstrations on his/ her own as well as providing background knowledge and skills for teaching.
- is able to utilize technology effectively in teaching and learning situations (See Jones, 2010).

The teacher is highly capable in using feedback from evaluation to assist each pupil to do well in ongoing lessons and units of study. Mandated tests, teacher observation, valid and reliable teacher written tests, supervisory visits, pupil and teacher self evaluation results, rating scales, checklists, among others should provide information/data on necessary steps to help learners individually to achieve well. Motivated pupils, actively interested in achieving, need to ascertain meaning and purpose in optimizing learner progress.

REFERENCES

Bybee, R. W. (1997), *Achieving Scientific Literacy*. Portsmouth, New Hampshire: Heinemann.

Ediger, Marlow, and D. Bhaskara Rao (2010), *School Science Curriculum*. New Delhi, India: Discovery Publishing House.

Ediger, Marlow (2010), *"Children's Literature in the Science Curriculum,"* Journal of Instructional Psychology," 37 (2), 117-119.

Jones, Alex D. (2010), *"Science Via Photography,"* Science and Children, 47 (5), 26-30.

Martinez, Monica (2010), *"Teacher Education Can't Ignore Technology,"* Phi delta Kappan, 92 (2), 74-75.

National Research Council (1996), *National Science Education Standards*. Washington DC: National Academy Press.

CHAPTER 18

Reading Critically in Science Curriculum

With the tremendous emphasis placed upon reading in the educational literature and in the news, it behooves science teachers to place heavy stress upon achievement in this curriculum area. Mandated testing has been strong on evaluating reading progress. High stakes testing, therein, puts reading on a pedestal for learner achievement. Teachers have been pressured to teach more reading due to its importance in testing situations. Reading then needs to be included in each curriculum area, science included. To be sure, there is much reading in science and it can make its numerous contributions to learner success. However, individual differences do need to be provided for with the diverse interests, purposes, and abilities involved (Ediger, 2007). What might the science teacher do to encourage pupil achievement in critical reading?

Helping Pupils to Succeed in Reading

The science teacher needs to be a teacher of reading well as of academic content in earth, physical, and life sciences which provide content for the science. If basal textbooks are used in teaching, the teacher must be certain that new learnings are based upon what pupils have achieved previously. This is an important factor in teaching which might well make for pupil success in achievement. The new and the old just previously learned should be seamless in sequence. Failure occurs in learning if the new subject matter is too complex to master or if the content is too easy which might well make for boredom in learning. Challenging facts, concepts, and generalizations may be acquired through scaffolding. Thus, the teacher assists each pupils to attain what otherwise might be too difficult (Ediger 2006). This might well be illustrated with the new vocabulary to be introduced to learners prior to their reading from the basal science textbook. These should be neatly printed on the experience chart which all can see clearly. The words need to be meaningfully defined and/or used within sentences to fit the contextual use in the textbook. The science teacher assists pupils to bridge the gap between previous and the ensuing subject matter. What pupils know about vocabulary might then be extended to what they will be reading from the textbook. Contextual illustrations from the text need to be utilized to help learners attach meaning to the new vocabulary. Illustrations from the teacher's file as well as in a video tape may further illuminate understanding. Accuracy in meaning separates what is correct from the vague and the hazy (Ediger 2010).

Assessing the topical headings in the reading selection should aid pupils in providing readiness for comprehension. They need to be turned into questions; necessary information might then be gleaned to secure answers. It is wise to provide readiness experiences, prior to pupils reading the textbook selection. Reading critically may then be in evidence.

During this time, pupils should be encouraged to raise questions which provide an additional framework for seeking answers during the ensuing science reading experience (See DeRoche and Kostelny).

Followup activities should consist of in-depth discussions. Here, pupils need to read critically to separate accurate from inaccurate information, as well as facts from opinions. Then too, reading between the lines is salient since not all content might not or cannot be written with precise language. Metaphors and similes are a case at point. When these are used, a discussion should clarify intent.

When supervising university student teachers in the public schools, the writer observed several lessons taught with pupil contributions coming from library books largely. The unit emphasized prehistoric life and the age of dinosaurs. The topic is generally very interesting to pupils and the ensuing discussion was vibrant indeed. Pupils obtained library book content on the plesiosaur/mosasur, the tyrannosaurus rex, the diplodocus, the stegosarus, duck billed dinosaurs, among others. Illustrations were shown of each which was followed, in sequence, by a video tape to further clarify ideas and extend meanings. A myriad of questions were raised and committees formed to answer questions and solve problems such as the following:

- were most dinosaurs warm or cold blooded? What major differences would this make?
- why weren't a few dinosaurs saved from the catastrophic event of their annihilation?
- why did the archaeptorex possess claws on its wings?

Committees gathered data which was then presented to the class.

Enthusiasm tends to be high when learners themselves identify and solve dilemmas experienced. Art work was brought in to the unit with committees making models contained in the ongoing unit of study. Thus, from lightly soaked paper towels, a committee made a sea turtle from the Mesozoic era. The turtle was molded from the paper toweling and let to dry. Tempera paint used to show specific features of the model turtle made helped make for motivating displays of art work (See Parker, 2001).

Children's literature can make for valuable contributions in pupil learning. They may be displayed at an interest center from which pupils might browse and select to read. If pupils find the contents of interest, they tend to choose other interesting books for personal reading. These may be of the same/similar author or genre. Pupils must practice much reading in order to improve skills as well as increase knowledge. Achievement is cumulative and it contributes to further growth and progress. Knowledge and skills presently acquired provide building blocks for ensuing achievement.

A free reading time might also be in the offing whereby learners select sequential library books to read. If a pupil is unable to settle down to reading a book, the teacher needs to assist and offer guidance in sustained silent reading. He/she may pronounce unidentified words, as needed, to pupils during this time. Ideas gleaned may be brought into ongoing discussions in the unit being studied.

Peer reading can be beneficial in that pupils in the small group read from the same book and assist each other to develop higher levels of cognition as well as with word recognition. Reciprocal reading might also be stressed here with peers taking turns reading the content aloud. Then too, oral reading may be emphasized when a peer member lacks necessary reading skills. The latter should follow along, viewing the printed words in the book, as the reading aloud activity continues. Children must be encouraged to checkout library books to read at home. There are myriad ways of assisting pupils to read and analyze books with critical reading.

One more idea pertaining to encouraging reading, the writer observed a co-operating/student teacher read aloud during story hour which related to the ongoing unit of study. These teachers in a conference mentioned that pupils would later read the same titles in spare school time. Reading skills and critical thinking improved in the curriculum over time (See Stiggins, 1997).

Writing in the Science Unit of Study

There are a plethora of ways to utilize abstract content read in a unit of study. One way is to emphasize a hands on approach in learning through constructing a model our doing an experiment. This requires careful planning, implementation of the plans, and evaluation of the completed product. Hands on procedures in learning opportunities assists in providing for individual differences in interests, talents, and abilities among pupils.

Abstract activities also may be implemented to help pupils use what has been acquired through reading from the basal textbook and library books, among other media. The teacher needs to model developmentally appropriate tasks so that learners understand what is being emphasized. The latter should always be guided to perceive purpose in the writing experience. It should not be that writing is stressed for the sake of doing so, but there are practical reasons for becoming a good writer, useful in school and in society. Which kinds of written works are salient? The following are recommended:

- summaries. Pupils need assistance to summarize what has been read. The summary must pay attention to major ideas as well as subordinate content, otherwise there is a lack of organization in the written product. Topic sentences to begin with in written instruction should orientate the reader of the summary to ensuing subject matter. Pupils may be lead through what are major as well as subordinate ideas. The balance of the summary supports the topic sentence or main idea. Pupils, too, need help in sequencing the subordinate ideas. Pupils should be lead through the order here and change/ modify what must be altered in subsequent content. Critical thinking is inherent (See Shareeja, 2010).
- outlines. Through outlining content, pupils are aided in noting the orderly progression in writing. The teacher

may begin here by discussing sequence within an outline containing blank spaces. Thus, the topic sentence is given and pupils need to fill in one or two subordinate ideas with one already provided. If details are to be added, the science teacher may omit one detail with pupils determining the other subsequent ideas in sequence. All of the preceding parts of an outline might come from a section in the basal science textbook. Pupils with teacher guidance may then check for accuracy of the outline with the comparison made.

- diary entries. Each learner needs to keep dated diary entries of subject matter acquired as well as skills attained. This helps pupils to note major ideas attained as well as those of lesser significance. Practice in writing is then stressed, along with the other forms of written work state above.
- log entries. These are to be emphasized so that pupils learn to combine diary entries into an organized whole. The entries are good to use for review purposes (Ediger, 2007).

The above writing activities assist pupils to read, proof read, and engage in critical thinking. The important ideas, always, must be separated from the less salient.

REFERENCES

DeRoche, and Susan J. Kostelny (2006), *"An Adventure in Problem Based Reading,"* Phi Delta Kappan, 87 (9),708-709.

Ediger, Marlow (2007), *"Meaning in Reading Instruction,"* Reading Improvement, 44 (4), 217-220.

Ediger, Marlow (2006), *"Scaffolding in the Reading Curriculum,"* Iowa Educational Leadership, 8 (4), 24-26.

Ediger, Marlow (2010), *"Issues in the Social Studies,"* International Journal of Research, Development, and Extension, 1 (1), 43-49.

Ediger, Marlow (2007), *Teaching Science in Elementary Schools*. New Delhi, India: Discovery Publishing House.

Parker, Walter C. (2001), *Social Studies in Elementary Education*. Upper Saddle River, New Jersey: Prentice Hall, Inc.

Shareeja, Ali M. C. (2010), *"Macognition: Concept and Development,"* Edutracks, 9 (9), 10-13.

Stiggins, Richard J. (1997), Student Centered Classroom Assessment. Upper Saddle River, New Jersey: Merrill.

Science Curriculum and Levels of Pupil Thinking

It is salient to develop pupils ability to think since this pervades all curriculum areas as well as in the societal domain. Too frequently, pupils achieve in the lowest level such as recall of information. The recall level is important and provides building blocks for higher levels of cognition. However, in school and in society, increasingly complex thinking patterns must be stressed. What might the science teacher do to implement these kinds of activities in the science curriculum?

Sequencing Diverse Levels of Thought

A variety of rich teaming experiences must be provided pupils to achieve vital objectives in science. These should be concrete, semi-concrete, and abstract in nature as well as provide for pupil optimal progress. Individually, each needs to attain as optimally as possible. Thus, for example within an ongoing unit of study, pupils need to carefully observe igneous, sedimentary, and metamorphic rocks, as concrete learning materials. They must feel and handle these specimens, using a magnifying glass. Here, pupils are learning facts at the *recall* level. Pupils, individually, may then recall and identify each type of rock. Additional experiences include seeing each of these rock classifications using a computerized projection on the white board, as well as on power point slides. With related discussions, pupils might infer characteristics of selected rocks (Ediger and Rao, 2010).

The level of *understanding* follows with pupils attaching meaning to how each of the three rock categories were formed. Here, the spoken voice may use verbal cues in teaching in that voice inflection is in evidence. Thus, appropriate enunciation, stress, and pitch of selected words assists learners in attending to ongoing presentations. The attention of pupils then is drawn toward how rocks are formed. A quality video tape together with the accompanying spoken voice, for example, may indicate clearly how sedimentary rock are formed in bodies of water by cementing small fragments of limestone, over time. Illustrations in the video tape provide visual cues in focusing learner attention on relevant content. Environmental cues further assist pupil understanding such as words on a word wall which pupils may refer/relate to for previous as well as ongoing concepts in an ensuing unit of study.

Reinforcement of learnings is in evidence with revisits to concepts and vocabulary previously studied. The science teacher may incorporate non-verbal clues within those clues previously mentioned by using hand motions as well as using facial expressions (nods of the head, smiles, and using eye contact) which encourage learning, the teacher maximizes pupil achievement (Ediger and Rao, 2002).

In an appropriate sequence, the level of *critical thinking* might well be stressed. The learner increasingly analyzes relevant for that which is not relevant to the topic or subject matter being discussed. Too frequently, pupils focus upon the trivial rather that what is essential to attach meaning. In discussing volcanic eruptions, for example, pupils might study lava and metamorphic rock, with clarification on their differences and how these were formed when uncovered from volcanic eruption. Elaboration goes further into topics of formation and involved differences. An indepth sequence is emphasized here. The science teacher always must be aware of sequence when elaborating to create elucidation of ideas. Otherwise, pupils may become lost in the shuffle (Frey and Fisher, 2010).

Synthesizing Information obtained stresses, among other things, for learners to attain conclusions and summaries. Pupils being able to synthesize accurately and holistically is salient in every day studies in school as well as in the societal arenas. A summary/conclusion must contain vital gleaned information, with no room for fragmented content. It may be compared to the central idea which, in one sentence, states saliency of subject matter in a toad topic sentence within a paragraph/summary. The teacher in sequence may have pupils read silently a selection from the basal science textbook on the utilization of rocks and minerals after which the teacher models aloud how to arrive at a summary. Learners must notice carefully the order of content used here. This may be followed with modeling of the central idea. Pupils might then read aloud, in turn, subject matter on soil erosion. Reading fluently and with prosody acquires pupil attention and develops proficiency in comprehension, as well as in thinking about a conclusion. The conclusion, as well as the previously mentioned summary, must hold water in that each has supporting details (Tiedt, 1982).

Creative thought stresses the importance of developing unique, novel ideas. Creative ideas helps a society to move forward from where it is presently to something new which improves, beautifies, and enhances. Poetry is one avenue of creative expression and these poems may be written in different forms. Thus, acquired science subject matter may be written with rhyme such as:

- a couplet with two lines rhyming
- triplets with three lines rhyming
- quatrains with four lines of rhymed verse
- limericks with lines one, two, and five rhyming, as well as lines three and four with rhyme.
- haiku with five, seven, five syllables respectively per line
- tanka with five, seven, five, seven, seven syllables sequentially per line
- free verse with no set number of lines or syllables, nor of length.

Acrostic poems are fascinating for numerous pupils to write. Thus, the pupil may take any vocabulary term from the science unit being studied and write it vertically, with continuance in writing a phrase or sentence such as in the following:

Erosion
Engraven in soil and rocks
Riding in force with wind or water
Often appearing in time on the earth's surface
Softens as well as hardens by forces of nature
Inbedded in the weathering process
On the surface of the earth
Nature's way of telling a story (Ediger, 2010).

Creative stories, art products, among others, are good to emphasize in teaching science. Ingredients may be added such as alliteration which contains two or more successive words beginning with the same sound.

Information based library books might well interest pupils in a specific topic in science. In a unit on Desert Life, for instance, there are a plethora of library books written on different reading levels for children. The learner may select sequential books to read which capture his/her attention and these might well be used to supplement discussions in an ongoing science unit of study. In several classes observed by the author, when supervising university student teachers, pupil discussion on desert fife was based entirely from library book content. Each contributed in an atmosphere of respect. This might well be a method of varying the kinds of learning opportunities for pupils, along with science experiments, demonstrations, AV aids, oral reports, portfolios, writing experiences, and the use of computers and technology (See National Science Education Standards, 1996).

REFERENCES

Ediger, Marlow, and D. Bhaskara Rao (2010), *School Science Education*. New Delhi, India: Discovery Publishing House.

Ediger, Marlow, and D, Bhaskara Rao (2002), *Philosophy and Curriculum*. New Delht, India: Discovery Publishing.

Ediger, Marlow (2010), *"Children's Literature in the Science Curriculum."* Reading Improvement, 37 (2), 117-119.

Frey, Nancy, and Douglas Fisher, (2010), *"Identifying Instructional Moves During Guided Learning,"* The Reading Teacher, 64 (2), 84-95.

National Science Education Standards (1996). National Research Council.

Tiedt, Iris M. (1982), *Language Arts Handbook*. Englewood Cliffs, New Jersey: Prentice-Hall, Inc.

Children's Literature and Science Curriculum

A quality children's literature programme needs to be correlated with ongoing science lessons and units of study. It can enhance and enrich the science curriculum. Pupils tend to enjoy reading library books and the literature may assist pupils to explore topics in greater depth. In addition to science experiments, demonstrations, and multi-media, children's literature is another avenue of learning science concepts and generalizations. Voluntarily, pupils may pursue personal interests and purposes in science (Ediger and Rao, 2005).

Children's Literature and Science

An attractive bulletin board display showing selected book jackets of new library books should be readily visible to children in the classroom. The science teacher needs to refer to the bulletin board while introducing library books to the class. This provides readiness for choosing a library book to read. Subject matter presented provides background information for reading. Pupils then have an overview of content in a library book, making it easier to comprehend. During spare time in the school day, pupils may read science content. While supervising university student teachers in the public schools, the writer experienced the use of library book content in a science lesson discussion. Thus instead of using the basal text, pupils presented ideas on "The Changing Surface of the Earth" from related library book content. The discussion was engaging and lively with comments from almost each pupil. Smaller groups make it possible for more frequency of participation by each child and this was observed in a different observational visit. A good library of science books is a must! It is a way of further securing pupil interest in different topics in science (Ediger, 2007-2008).

There are more approaches in stressing children's literature in science. During story time, the teacher needs to read aloud to pupils carefully chosen library books on science content. He/she needs to read with voice inflection, appropriate pitch, and enunciation. Obtaining and maintaining learner attention is important. If children are of primary school age, it is good to show the related illustrations as content is being read orally. This assists these young children to understand subject matter read. The speed of oral reading needs to engage good listening. Periodically, the teacher needs to ask interesting questions pertaining to content read. These questions and forthcoming answers might well propel pupils to acquire further information on their own (Ray, 2006).

The content read aloud may motivate pupils to select a problem area to solve. The problem takes time to solve and involves deliberation and time to secure necessary information. The library books, science experiments, and the internet, among other reference sources, may be used. Critical thinking needs to be emphasized in separating facts from opinions, fantasy from reality, and accurate from inaccurate content. Objective information then needs to be secured. Individual or small group endeavours may be involved in problem solving. Creative thinking, too, may be stressed in coming up with new solutions to problems. Creative thinking also needs to be encouraged because improvements in school and in society come about due to novel, unique ideas developed. Thus, library books read to children do help learners to branch out in their thinking (National Research Council, 1996).

As another science library book activity, a certain period of time needs to be set aside during the school day for pupils to read a self selected library book. Generally, a pupil will choose a book of personal interest and on his/her reading level. Pupils tend to select sequential library books which are meaningful and they perceive purpose in their reading. Individualized reading motivates learners to read since they have personal ownership due self selection of reading materials. Developing a life long interest in reading and learning about science is salient (See American Association for the Advancement of Science, 1993).

When peers read a science library book together and share its contents, they may well engage in higher levels of cognition since ideas circulate among participants. Vygotsky (1978) advocated a social situation in learning whereby ideas "bounce off the minds of participants" and are scaffolded. Scaffolding occurs when content is too difficult to understand but is achievable with smaller sequential steps of learning. The sequential steps of learning are based upon the pupil's previous knowledge and lead to the initial complex idea. Science teachers, too, may use scaffolding in teaching by identifying an idea not understood but achievable through smaller ordered learning activities. These order steps of learning are based upon what pupils do understood, leading to the more complicated learning. When pupils in a committee setting see illustrations in a library book, they decide what they already know about the topic. It assists pupils to integrate and use previous knowledge to predict what will transpire. Also, pupils raise questions for which they may read the ensuing library book to secure answers. These experiences aid in comprehending more fully of what will be read (See Luchmann, 2007).

Extending learnings here might involve doing a project for a science fair or for an ongoing science unit of study. The writer has served as a judge at numerous science fairs and feels positive about many projects appraised. The projects are an outgrowth of the science curriculum, student independent reading, interests, and thought. Along with the quality of the project, the writer looked for and evaluated the following:

- where the idea came from for the construction of the project. It is good if the ideas come from the learner, meaning it is not dictated by parents or the teacher. However, support by both is important
- the care with which sequential steps in planning the project were stressed
- the purpose of the project
- the hypotheses to be tested in the project
- sources of information used.

A few of the projects evaluated included solar panels, a model of the solar system, control of wind and water erosion of soil, a model earthquake structure, a system of wind energy, and a model flood control project (See Bowers, 2005).

Communicating with Parents

In a quality science programme of instruction, it is good to develop and maintain open lines of communication with parents. The children's literature programme is no exception. The school reading programme needs to be connected with that of the home. E-mail, face to face meetings, and the voice recorder may be used as media for the messages. Both science teacher and parents need to exchange messages pertaining to:

- pupil interest and general progress made in reading.
- pupil achievement in comprehension, including higher levels of cognitio.
- pupil mastery of word recognition skills.
- pupil problems in reading fluently.
- pupil skills in working with others in co-operative learning (Ediger, 2008).

Personal achievement is important for each pupil. Pupils individually must learn to monitor their very own progress. This means that the child is not a word caller, but checks the self to ascertain personal comprehension as the act of reading continues. Thus, the learner can then say aloud and attach meaning to content read. Comprehension is the objective in reading science subject matter (See Hansen, 2003).

REFERENCES

American Association for the Advancement of Science (1993), Benchmarks for Science Literacy. New York: Oxford University Press.

Bowers, Susan (2005), *"The Portfolio Process: Questions for Implementation and Practice,"* The College Student Journal, 39 (4), 754-758.

Ediger, Marlow, and D. Bhaskara Rao (2005), *Teaching Science in Elementary Schools.* New Delhi, India: Discovery Publishing House.

Ediger, Marlow (2008), *"Student Vocabulary Development in the Science Curriculum,"* Connecticut Journal of Science Education, 45 (1), 12-13.

Ediger, Marlow, *"Psychology of Parental Invovlement in Reading,"* Reading Improvement, 45 (1), 46-52.

Luchmann, A. L. (2007), *"Identity Development as a Lens to Science Teacher Preparation, Science Education"*, 91, 822-839.

Hansen, Laurie (2003), *"Science in any Language,"* Science and Children, 41 (3), 35-39.

National Research Council (1995), National Science Education Standards, Washington DC: National Academy Press.

Ray, Katie Wood (2006), *"What Are You Thinking?"* Educational Leadership, 64 (2), 58-62.

Vygotsky, L. S. (1978), *Mind in Society: The Development of Higher Psychological Processes.* Cambridge, Massachusetts: Harvard University Press.

CHAPTER 21

Pointers in Teaching Social Studies

A Quality Social Studies Curriculum is needed to assist pupils to do well in relating well to others in School and in Society. Multiculturalism needs to be emphasized in ongoing lessons and units of study due to a society which has numerous ethnic groups and nationalities. Thus, there are a plethora of cultural groups which need to be studied so that learners experience positive interactions, feelings, and acceptance. Pupils in the school setting need to be grouped so that maximum collaboration is possible.

Encouraging Multicultural Experiences

Increasingly, public schools have pupils who speak another language than English. When entering first grade in 1934, the writer spoke low German largely. In his Mennonite church affiliation, the language of the church was high German. As early as 1950, English largely became a predominate language of the church. The appearance of men and women then and now were/are exactly like other people in society including hair styles, suits and dresses. Change, in many factors, was somewhat rampant, although selected cultural factors, in degrees, remained such as the following:

- being in alternative rather than military service in times of conscription. Although, there were individuals who entered military service.
- being a farming population; however, this is changed dramatically due to a lack of farm land and farming opportunities. Rural culture, however, remains salient.
- living in a homogeneous community. Presently, many different vocations, occupations, and professions are being followed whereby people tend to move to areas where work opportunities are such as in urban and suburban areas.

A more stable society, with less change, are the Old Order Amish. They use horse and carriage for transportation rather than modern vehicles. Those who farm, less than twenty five per cent do, use draft horses instead of tractors. Grain drills pulled by horses are used for crop seeding as wells harrows and disks for soil tilling. There are a few Amish communities which operate tractors for pulling farm implements. These may be used, too, for going into town for buying needed goods. Grain binders and threshing machines are used for harvesting crops rather than self propelled combines with air conditioned cabs. Married women are house wives and take care of the home and family, generally with five or six children. There are a few exceptions such as a rural grocery store being operated by an Amish family. Amish men have entered into a variety kinds of occupations such as construction work, the making of furniture, and repair work on small engines.

The same pattern of dress is inherent for Amish Women with high necklines, long sleeves which go down to the wrist, and length of dress extending to the ankles. Amish men wear beards, have suspenders for holding up trousers, wear black suits for Sunday services with no ties. All clothing for men and women as well as for children possess a plain colour, not stripes nor checks in design.

Amish children go to school for eight years which is terminal. Usually, these are parochial schools operated by the Old Order Amish with teachers of their own faith doing the teaching. Generally, these are Amish women who teach. Textbooks used may be from leading publishing companies; however, basals from the Rod and Staff Publishing Company may be utilized containing sequential phonic lessons and biblical stories such as biographies of Abraham, Lot, Isaac, and Jacob, among others. Mathematics is a secular subject and the MacMillan, Harcourt Brace and World, or other publishing companies provide subject matter content in these textbooks. Social studies content comes from subject matter contained from a secular publishing company. Grammar is emphasized heavily in written work, that tends to stress factual, not creative content.

Recess time may consists of playing softball, volley ball, and croquet when the weather is favourable. In cold weather, if there is an ice pond or creek near the school building, ice skating is popular. Running games like tag, handi-over, and 23 eskadoo are also popular in winter. Otherwise, Amish children stay indoors on cold days and play quiz games or checkers/dominos. The internet contains much information on the Amish as well as other Mennonite groups. Reference sources for children's and adult library books are given pertaining to these cultural societies.

Multi-cultural Activities in the Social Studies

As the name indicates, multicultural education emphasizes diverse ethnic as well as minority groups for studying. There are a plethora of Latinos in society. These may speak Spanish, largely or only. They possess salient customs, religious beliefs, as well as philosophies of life. These need to be pinpointed as vital objectives of instruction in an integrated social studies curriculum. Learning opportunities need to be selected in order that learners might achieve the chosen objectives. Video tapes, musical recordings, digital and actual Latino art work, architecture such as large Catholic cathedrals, need to be studied and appreciated, native foods eaten (there are, of course numerous Mexican restaurants in society serving authentic foods), native folk dances may be taught, as well as important facets of the Spanish language such as greetings used. Learning opportunities then must be accurate, authentic, as well as valid and reliable. Pupils need to have ample opportunities to interact with diverse minority groups in favourable situations whereby positive feelings are developed among Latinos, as well as African Americans.

In studying an integrated with other primary and secondary cultures, African American culture needs to stress harmonious relationships with others. Good will and positive human relationships need achieving. Respect and caring are salient features to become a part of each social studies unit of study. Knowledge, skills, and attitudinal ends need careful attention so that representative cultural factors pertaining to African Americans are forth coming. African American content must emphasize leaders in American society such as The Rev. Al Sharpton, Rev. Jesse Jackson, the late Supreme Court Justice Thurgood Marshall, the late Rosa Parks, writer Angelou Mayou, and President Barak Obama. There are many athletes such as Mohammed Ali and Kobe Bryant, as well as actors/entertainers who have been/are famous such as the late Michael Jackson.

The literary works, art products, music, architecture, foods, and the many other accomplishments of African Americans need to be studied and become a salient part of the pupil's repertoire.

A multicultural social curriculum is needed in order that pupils understand the many contributions made by Latinos, African Americans, native Americans, as well as Jewish Americans. My own experiences lead me to the Middle East in the early 1950s in alternative to military service. On the

West Bank of the Jordan, then a part of the nation of Jordan, one of us assisted in clothing distributions in Palestinian refugee camps. The clothing distributions, in general, were orderly. These people lived in clay huts with thatched roofs and no sanitation facilities in Aqaba Camp, directly south of Jericho. Their food consisted of United Nations rations for refugees. Water was generally carried in clay pots from Ein Sultan or Elisha's fountain in Jericho, four miles away.

One of us also taught at Friends Boys School, a boarding school for boys, located in Ramallah. Approximately, half were Muslims whereas the other half were Greek and Armenian Orthodox Christians. Any major differences in school behaviour among the different groups was not noticed. Pupils should have opportunities to visit with and interact with people of Muslim Beliefs. This needs to be done in a positive atmosphere whereby acceptance is a key concept. Essential beliefs of Muslims for pupils to study are the following:

- after performing ablutions, they pray five times a day at prescribed times and with proper postures, facing Mecca, Saudi Arabia, the birth place of their prophet Mohammed.
- once in a life time, devout followers of Islam make a required trip to Mecca, during Ramadan, and thus receive the title Hajj. There are exceptions to this rule, such as a person having ill health.
- the Muslim creed is recited at prayer time—There is no God, but one God, and Mohammed is His prophet
- the Quar'an is the Holy book of Islam and devout followers generally worship in a Mosque. A nearby minaret is used by the leader, known as an Imam, to call people to prayer.
- titles are given to the poor and less fortunate such as two and one half per cent of one's wealth, annually.

With an increased population of Muslims and the building of Mosques, it behooves schools to implement quality units of study on Islam. Less than thirty miles from my home is a Muslim school for children, on the northern outskirts of Wichita, Kansas. The school building represents the likeness of the Dome of the Rock, a beautiful, octagonal mosque, inside the walls of the walled city of Jerusalem. This mosque was built in 691 AD, and is the third holiest site of Islam, with Mecca being the holiest, followed by Medina, 200 miles to the north and containing the tomb of Mohammed (570-632 AD).

A very rich cultural experience, for the writer, was to eat meals with nomads (bedouin). Bedouin tents were located outside of Jericho, the West Bank. The temperature is mild in winter, above freezing, but is warm from January to October with extremely hot temperature readings—April through August. Bedouin men sit in one side of the tent and the women in the other. I sat with men for eating, squatted on the ground. The hands were used for eating rice and lamb's meat, the latter reserved for special occasions, from a metal platter. It is truly a skill to eat using the hands. Furniture and utensils are kept to an extreme minimum due to the necessity of moving to where the grass is suitable for grazing by sheep, goats, camels, and donkeys. Bedouin hospitality is excellent due to the respect for visitors.

In addition to first hand experiences with diverse cultural groups, reading from internet, viewing video tapes, reading library books as well as content from basal textbooks, there are numerous rich construction experiences emphasizing eye/hand co-ordination which extend previous learnings obtained. These include the following:

- making a model cloth tent, paper mache' desert animals, and clay figures of bedouins.
- scrolls as used in the Roman Empire, as well as bound booklets of compiled children's stories written in ongoing lessons and units of study.

- musical flutes as used by bedouins for entertainment when herding sheep and goats. The flute may consist of a paper tube coming from the inside of a role of paper toweling with small openings made along the tube. Air may then be blown in from a flattened sturdy card board mouth piece. The fingers are utilized to open and close these holes, making for different levels of pitch.
- a small scale Dome of the Rock, representing a Mosque inside the walled city of Jerusalem. My grandson, for example, made a model ancient Greek parthenon in an ongoing sixth grade unit of study.
- a "television set" consisting of a cardboard box with an open front. Two wooden dowel rods may be inserted into the cardboard box with a roll of butcher paper around these rods. The butcher paper needs to be flat on the floor or desk top so that illustrations and related wording might be printed thereon. The butcher paper is then placed around the dowel rods of the "television set" for a committee of pupils to tell and show the story of the segment of the social studies unit taught.
- sock puppets which pertain to multi-cultural experiences such as decorating a sock with costumes pertaining to people of the middle East. These may then be used to tell a story of an ongoing lesson or unit of study.
- making and using a loom to make cloth as bedouins do in a tent setting.
- doing a relief map made of an equal mixture of flour and salt and enough water to hold the ingredients together to show vital cities/features such as Tel Aviv, Cairo, Jerusalem, Ammon, Damascus, Baghdad, the Judean Hills, The Sea of Galilee, Dead Sea, among others. The relief map should be tempera painted with a legend to show elevation.
- shape clay animals such as sheep and goats as well as into pottery to hold water.

- make a mural showing the walled city of Jerusalem, the Church of the Holy Sepulcher, the Mosque El Aqsa (adjacent to the Dome of the Rock), and the Western wall, a holy place for devout followers of Judaism.

The above are examples of hands on approaches in teaching and learning situations in the social studies. Additional learning opportunities include the following, among others:

- use of reading materials involving basal textbooks, library books, internet sources, newspapers and newsmagazines.
- video tapes, CDs and DVDs, as well as transparencies and the overhead projector.
- power point presentations, slides, and illustrations.
- single concept film loops and tape recordings.
- quality resource personnel.

It is salient to provide for the talents and abilities of each pupil. Pupils possess different styles of learning and each must achieve as optimally as possible.

CHAPTER 22

Psychology of Learning and Teaching Social Studies

The social studies teacher must use the psychology go learning in planning and implementing the curriculum. This assists pupils to achieve more optimally. Motivating disinterested pupils, who have little purpose in achieving stated objectives, with stimulating learning opportunities, aids learners to develop, attain, and grow. Quality attitudes should be an end result of achievement. They facilitate learners in developing an inward desire to learn. Too frequently, there is a low energy level for learning on the part of some pupils. Achievement then tends to move in a negative direction. The social studies teacher must possess a repertoire of knowledge and skills in helping pupils to attain objectives (Ediger, 2010).

Intrinsic Versus Extrinsic Motivation

Intrinsic motivation emphasizes that pupils have an inward desire to learn. Pupils are interested in learning more about each social studies lesson and unit being pursued. On their own as well as with teacher guidance, pupils gather information in subject matter content. The sky may well be the limit in learning in these situations. It would be good if all pupils have this inward motivation. There are teaching suggestions in facilitating inward motivation with the following:

- change the learning activity before pupils become disinterested.
- modulate the teacher's speaking voice so that appropriate pitch, stress, and enunciation secures learner attention.
- have adequate pupil input into the lesson/unit of study by raising stimulating questions.
- develop active pupil involvement in the social studies.
- use committee endeavours as well as individual work.
- provide pupil choice, at intervals, in terms of which tasks learners would desire to accomplish (See Ritchhart and Perkins, 2008).

Extrinsic motivation, also, has its advocates. The social studies teacher then uses external factors in motivating pupils. For example, the teacher might motivate extrinsically by giving praise judiciously to work well done*. This should spur pupils on to desiring praise with continuous achievement. The following additional examples are provided:

- providing time for free choice of activity following one or more tasks well done.
- having a popcorn party, Friday afternoon when pupils meet definite, high criteria in learning. The criteria are established prior to pupils working on achieving them.
- giving an inexpensive prize for attaining a specific goal in a social studies lesson.

The token economy or direct giving of a prize is utilized for work well done where the standards were stated prior to the announcement of the award. The social studies teacher must decide, here, under what conditions a prize is to be given (Ediger, 2009).

Sequence in Learning

Who largely should determine sequence in learning? Toward one end of the continuum, the teacher might choose in which order learning opportunities are to be provided for pupils. Here, the social studies teacher studies pupils, individually, to ascertain sequence. He/she must choose that which assists pupils to achieve optimally. The learning opportunities must not be too complex to preordain failure or so easy that learners feel bored. Scaffolding might be used, where feasible, in ongoing lessons and units of study. A variety of kinds of activities may well be used to provide for individual differences in growth, attainment, and progress. The teacher attempts to secure the interests and purposes of pupils in teaching and learning situations. Success in learning is always salient (See, National Council for the Social Studies, 1997).

Toward the other end of the continuum, the teacher may serve as a guide and facilitator of learning. A learning stations procedure might be utilized. The teacher or teacher/pupil planning may be used in developing four stations, for example, with five tasks for pupils to select from at each station. There are more tasks than pupils can complete so that those most appealing might be chosen sequentially. The teacher introduces each station to pupils in a stimulating learning environment, which may consist of a bulletin board, a word wall, a mural, a video presentation, among others. Pupils, individually, might then select sequential tasks to work on, be they individual or committee endeavours. The learner ascertains sequence within the learning activity when making these choices. For example, the pupil might choose to make a model and with the available necessary materials order his/her own experiences with teacher help as needed. The model may pertain to developing a medieval manor. Otherwise, the pupil is free to pursue in the planning and executing of the task. The teacher scaffolds when needed to aid pupil achievement. Encouragement is used to enhance achievement. The final product is evaluated in terms of desired standards (See, Parker, 2001).

Perhaps, both teacher determined as well as a pupil centered procedure should be used in the social studies. This aids in providing for the needs, interests, and purposes of learners, individually as well as collectively.

A Subject Centered Versus an Activity Centered Curriculum

The psychology of learning involved here pertains to essential content, as determined by academicians, to be learned within a unit of study as compared to pupil purpose/ input in ongoing units of study. With essential subject matter, pupils acquire major concepts and generalizations as identified by social scientists in history, geography, economics, political science, as well as anthropology/sociology. The subject matter to be acquired by pupils is deemed necessary to become a good citizen as well as to be an informed person in school and in society. The social studies teacher explains to pupils what is not understood or is rather vague in the minds of learners. There are selected video tapes which can truly make learnings meaningful to pupils, such as one on the Renaissance period of time viewed by the writer. Here, pupils may view clothing worn, means of transportation, building of churches, university buildings, and the manor. Visual and related audio aids help pupils to attach meaning to historical and and social science concepts and generalizations (See, Fosnot, 1996).

Acquiring basic subject matter can be vitalized and meaningful to pupils.

Toward the other end of the continuum, social studies teachers feel that pupils learn facts, vocabulary, and main ideas through a learning by doing approach. A hands on procedure is then being emphasized. Salient subject matter is then learned at the time that a construction or art product is being created. Careful planning is necessary to develop and complete the ensuing product. Evaluation in terms of desirable criteria is used to assess its worth and neatness. To construct a model Parthenon, of ancient Athens, pupils need to see models, have the needed materials, and do meticulous work. The making part becomes meaningless unless it is accompanied by indepth related knowledge. The teacher is a facilitator, but not a "sage on the stage." The writer viewed a model Parthenon at a social studies fair. The pupil was well versed in knowledge about the Parthenon and its history. He was able to tell clearly how it was made and the obstacles faced during its sequential development from cardboard. It is indeed fascinating for pupils to construct, design, and model (See Bain, 2004).

Most social studies teachers will use both a subject centered and learning by doing. It is important that pupils garner relevant abstract learnings in the social studies and for some it may mean making models, murals, relief maps, puppets, among others to portray concepts and generalizations from the different disciplines making up content in the social studies. Learning styles of pupils vary due to individual differences in interests, talents, and abilities.

Determining objectives prior to instruction has been quite common, especially with state and district wide stated goals. Generally, these are stated in measurable terms so that pupils can be certain if they have/have not achieved these ends of instruction. Tests are aligned with the objectives to measure pupil achievement. With mandated objectives and aligned test, pupil achievement may be measured through the use of multiple choice test results. Percentiles usually are given to show learner progress. High stakes tests and their results indicate if a pupil is to be promoted to the next grade level. How effective this procedure in teaching is depends upon the quality of the standards (objectives), the implemented learning opportunities to achieve the stated objectives, as well as the validity/reliability of the multiple choice test items. There are selected weaknesses in using this procedure of instruction:

- there is little opportunity for pupil involvement in the curriculum such as questions they may wish to have answered within a lesson.
- with the accountability movement, teaching to the test may become sacred. What is tested might be what is taught. Teachers are held accountable for pupil achievement based on standardized test results.
- stating all objectives prior to instruction is risky business, due to impairment of selected pupils in attaining these ends, especially when they are stated well ahead of and prior to instruction as well as being too complex to achieve.

Somewhat toward the other end of the continuum is to utilize teacher/pupil planning in the social studies. Planning effectively is a highly complex skill, useful in school and in society. Adequate background information is necessary to plan well. Thus, within an ongoing unit of study, pupils with teacher guidance may plan learning opportunities to accomplish open ended objectives. The following need planning:

- which activities should be offered? This may involve developing a time line, dramatizing events from history, giving an oral book report, doing an art project related to the unit being taught, peer/group, discussions, writing summaries and conclusions, among others.
- how should each activity be evaluated so that quality is in evidence? Pupils must become proficient in doing things well and with evaluation, the final process/ product might well show quality work.

Pupil responsibility is significant here. Pupils need to do the learning, and the teacher must provide encouragement and effective modeling.

Conclusion

The psychology of learning, applied to teaching and learning situations, assists pupils to achieve more optimally. Then too, humaneness is involved when pupils experience that which meets academic, social, emotional, and physical needs. Learnings then need to provide for individual differences and be:

- engaging and interesting.
- purposeful and relevant.
- motivating and encourage curiosity.

REFERENCES

Bain, K. (2004), *What the Best College Teachers Do.* Cambridge, Massachusetts: Harvard University Press.

Ediger, Marlow (2010), *"Issues in the Social Studies,"* International Journal of Educational Research, Development, and Extension, 1 (1), 43-49.

Ediger, Marlow (2009), *"Supervising the Student Teacher in the Public School,"* Education,130 (2), 251-254).

Fosnot, C. (1996), *Constructivism: Theory, Perspectives, and Practice.* New York: Teachers College Press.

National Council for the Social (1997), *Curriculum Standards for the Social Studies.* Edison, New York: Whitehurst and Clark.

Parker Walter C. (2001), *Social Studies in Elementary Education.* Upper Saddle River, New Jersey: Merrill, Prentice Hall.

Ritchhart, Ron, and David Perkins (2008), *"Making Thinking Visible,"* Educational Leadership, 65 (5), 57-63.

Reading Creatively in Social Studies

Creative reading in the social studies is important since much interpretation of concepts and generalizations are required. The social studies does not have the objectivity which science and mathematics content possess. To be sure, the social studies has its precise names, dates, and places, as well as geography containing parallels, meridians, longitude, and latitude on maps and globes with precision, but with events and happenings in foreign policy, for example, creative interpretations are necessary as well as actions therein. For example in viewing a solution to the Palestinian Arab/Israeli conflict over the land of Palestine, the conflict continues to linger on over the decades. There have been a plethora of solutions offered here, but none has been implemented/ worked. There is none in sight presently. Creativity is needed to solve problems in this case and a myriad of others (Ediger, 2003).

Reading Subject Matter Creatively

One must have adequate background information to come up with creative solutions to problems. Thus in reading from a carefully chosen basal, pupils must experience readiness. New subject matter learnings need to be related to previously acquired content. This should be done as seamlessly as possible. Thus, the social studies teacher needs to introduce new concepts for pupil viewing and discussing. This provides necessary background information for reading from the textbook. Thus, for example, the following must be seen in print so that they will be recognized in the ensuing reading experience:

- the land of Palestine. A map should clearly show the boundaries and neighbouring nations.
- Israel. With its present boundaries together with the occupied West Bank need to be seen by learners on a large map.
- Palestinian Arab refugees. These locations may be viewed on a map of Palestine together with refugee camps in Jordan, Egypt, Syria, and Lebanon.
- the Jordan River. This river separates the nations Jordan and Israel.
- the walled city of Jerusalem. This city has a surrounding wall two and one-half miles in length (Ediger, 2010).

Pupils need clarification of ideas when questions arise. Inductively the teacher assists pupils to develop knowledge and skills in these situations. If a question arises pertaining to the fundamental beliefs of Islam, the following questions might well lead to tentative answers:

- Why do devout followers make a pilgrimage once, as a minimum, during their lifetime to Mecca, Saudi, Arabia? Here, pupils may be guided to read about the birthplace of their Prophet Mohammed in 570 AD, his flight from enemies (the Hegira) to Medina where he was later entombed in 632 AD; in the meantime, he returned to his native Mecca. The recordings, in the Koran of Mohammed's messages, were received as he meditated in a cave just outside of Mecca. Additional information, from a variety of reference sources, may be added as needed to assist pupils in arriving at conclusions.

- Why do Imams call the faithful to prayer five times a day from a minaret?
- What is the importance of Mount Moriah, located inside the Dome of the Rock sacred to both Jews and Arabs?
- Why is the Church of the Holy Sepulchre sacred to devout followers of Christianity?

In each of the above, the social studies teacher needs to help, but not provide direct information to each question/ problem. Creativity is involved in finding unique solutions to problems. Developmentally appropriate assistance must be provided. *Scaffolding* is an excellent concept to use here in that the teacher might well guide pupils through small progressive steps to secure an answer. The scaffold moves a pupil from where he/she is in achievement presently to some reasonable higher expectation. The learner's own creative thought propels the individual to reach out and upward to a desired level of accomplishment. Success in achievement is salient when the self concept is involved in creative thought. Pupils also need to respect each others ideas in order for novel ideas to come forth. Ridiculing and rudeness have no roles to play in the social studies curriculum. They hinder in productivity of ideas. Creativity thrives when pupils feel free to think and then come up with unique ideas for problem solving (See Shanklin and Rhodes, 1989).

Brain storming is an excellent procedure to use in stimulating creativity. The more ideas presented, the better in brainstorming. For instance, pupils may be encouraged to come up with as many responses as possible for the following:

- Why do both Palestinian Arabs and Israel want to govern, within a state/nation, the land of Palestine?
- Why is most of the land of Palestine hilly and mountainous? The triangular shaped Plains of

Esdraelen in contrast, twenty by twenty by thirty miles, is quite level and free from protruding limestone rocks.

Motivating and assisting pupils when needed is important, but ideas must come from pupils when creative endeavours are being implemented. The social studies teacher must know at what point to intervene so that learners have needed knowledge to pursue ensuing thoughts (See, De Roche and Kostelay, 2006).

Written Work and Creativity

There are myriad ways in which pupils may proceed with writing activities. Poetry certainly can and does emphasize unique approaches in presenting ideas. The teacher needs to assist pupils to recognize what makes for each type of poem as the printed poem is compared with other types of verse. The following guidelines are provided for poetry writing:

- pupils inductively should attach meaning to each kind of poem.
- they need to observe carefully how the teacher models the writing of a poem being emphasized in the ongoing unit of study.
- the teacher must find motivating approaches in assisting pupils to write poetry enthusiastically.
- enjoyment of diverse forms of poetry is salient as well as pupils desiring to write different kinds of verse.
- liking novel, unique ideas is of utmost importance (Ediger, 2006).

There are selected pupils who prefer rhyme in verse such as is true in writing couplets (two lines with ending words rhyming), triplets (three lines with ending words rhyming), quatrains with all four lines having rhyme), and limericks (lines one, two, and five rhyme whereas lines three and four rhyme). (See Tiedt, 1982). As an example, the following triplet written by a sixth grader reveals ending words rhyming:

The City of Amman
It bustles with cars in a busy nation
With over one million people in population
It strives to grow even more as individuals show elation.

In each of these poems, pupils utilize acquired subject matter in writing verse. Syllabication might also be used in poetry writing such as haiku containing five, seven, five syllables respectively for each of three lines, whereas a tanka contains five, seven, five, seven, seven syllables respectively for each of five lines of verse. The following haiku, for instance, was also written by a pupil in grade six:

Bedouin in the Dessert
Living in black tents
With camels nibbling sagebrush
Hoping for a rain.

Alliteration may be inserted as words within any poem written. Thus two or more sequential words beginning with the same initial sound make for alliteration such as "Donkeys doing neighs." Imagery may also be added to a poem. Here, a creative comparison is made such as "Clear skies in a dessert look as if *perfection reigns in the universe.*" "Clear skies" is compared with "perfection in the the universe." Pupils enjoy making creative comparisons when the concept of "imagery" is being emphasized in reading and writing poetry. Social studies teachers need to stress diverse poetry concepts when reading poems aloud as well as writing them as models for all to see clearly in the classroom (See Palinscar, *et. al.,* 1986).

Free verse is easier to write with no rhyme, nor number of syllables, or number of lines per poem. One form of free verse is for pupils to write acrostic poems. For each poem, the social studies teacher needs to provide a good model and this may be done orally as learners listen and observe intently when the poem is printed. The writer when supervising university student teachers in the public schools notice a sixth grader who wrote the following acrostic choosing the word Jordan (printed vertically) a nation east of the Jordan River:

Jordan whose capital city is Amman
Olive trees produce well in the Mediteranean world
Rice is a leading food eaten.
Dead Sea water contains about 25 per cent salt content
A land of many hills and valleys as well as dessert
Nomads herd sheep and goats within a modern nation.

The above acrostic poem indicates the pupil has learned much about the Middle East area of the world. Each line states important information about the nation of Jordan. Novel drawings may also be made of poetry written as well as of other creative works such as a short novel or short story.

REFERENCES

De Roche, and Susan Kostelay (2006), *"An Adventure in Problem Based Learning,"* Phi Delta Kappan, 87 (9), 708.

Ediger, Marlow Ediger (2003), *Teaching Social Studies Successfully.* New Delhi, India: Discovery Publishing House.

Ediger, Marlow (2010), *"Issues in the Social Studies,"* International Journal of Educational Research, Development and Extension, 1 (1), 43-49.

Ediger, Marlow (2006), *"Testing Versus Portfolios to Assess Achievement,"* OASCD Journal, 13 (1), 31-32.

Palinscar, *et. al.,* (1986), *Teaching Reading As Thinking.* Alexandria, Virginia: Association for Supervision and Curriculum Development.

Shanklin, N.L. and L.K. Rhodes (1989), *"Comprehension Instruction in Sharing and Extending,"* The Reading Teacher, 42 (1) 496-500.

Tiedt, Iris M. (1982), *The Language Arts Handbook.* Englewood Cliffs, New Jersey: Prentice Hall, Inc.

Master's Degree in Education

There are selected individuals and groups who are critical of the master's degree in education. They believe that a teacher securing the degree does not result in improved instruction. Secretary of Education Arne Duncan, among others, has come out strongly against the Master's degree in education. He maintains it cannot be shown that having the advanced degree makes for a better teacher. This is indeed difficult to measure with many variables entering into the equation. For example, those who emphasize testing pupils who are taught with a Master's degree will not achieve any more than those pupils taught by teachers without a master's degree. This has never been substantiated and there are too many extraneous factors involved such as quality of pupils in one group as compared to the other or:

- a level playing field between the two groups in terms of technology used in teaching, updated textbooks, as well as library books available for pupils, among other materials/methods of instruction.
- quality of teachers used in the experimental study with other factors involved than the masters degree.

Analyzing Teaching

There is more involved in teaching than setting standards for pupils to attain. *No Child Left Behind (NCLB) and Common Core Standards Stress the importance of setting predetermined standards for all pupils to attain.* These standards are developed by those far removed from the local teaching scene. They emphasize academic subject matter to be tested only. A major problem pertains to, "Have these standards been proven in terms of relevancy for learners in the school/community setting?" Are there others which would be more important to attain? Tests are very expensive to write with adequate validity and reliability. These tests must be pilot tested to notice if they possess *validity* and if they measure consistently to ascertain *reliability*. The Common Core Standards are the latest to be or are in the writing. It so happens that previous plans for curriculum improvement, like NCLB, become outdated and new programmes are entertained, such as tests for Common Core Standards. Much of the money used in developing these tests could be used to supply innovative technology, among other items, for curriculum improvement.

Second, are these reasonable standards for pupil achievement? Standards may be too complex or too easy for learner attainment. To feel successful, pupils should be able to achieve these standards with reasonable effort. Scaffolding may be emphasized to assist learners to attain at a higher level of cognition, but still there needs to be the possibilities of goal achievement. Those who criticize school achievement view test results only to measure progress, and then make negative comments about the results such as that "that is not good enough", or if the gaps between the majority and minority groups have not been eliminated. Rarely do outsiders look at the many variables affecting pupil achievement. All pupils are to attain the same standards including English Language Learners, special needs children, as well as those from minority groups. And yet, there is a great deal of difference in background experiences of these learners. For example, a child from a low income neighbourhood where drug dealings are prevalent and a high crime rate exists may have little chance of doing well in school. The surrounding environment then is not conducive to doing well in school as well as in society.

Schools of education offering a master's degree can emphasize training and experiences whereby an inservice teacher may receive professional guidance in methods courses and internships to overcome challenging teaching situations. These professors generally have years of teaching experience in the public schools and in professional education including the doctorate.

Third, does teaching to the test become the goal rather than are pupils learning? If mandated tests must be passed by learners in order to be promoted to the next higher grade level, high stakes are involved for both the pupil and the public school teacher with neither one desiring to fail. There is much tension and anxiety on the part of the involved pupil and his/her teacher. Might this energy be saved more so for teaching and learning situations. More emphasis should be placed upon the teacher through observation appraising the learner in all dimensions, especially, the academic, the social, and the emotional facets of development. Thus, the observant teacher can provide immediate assistance if pupils, for example, are not able to identify a word in reading. Or, pupils who do not get along with others might well be assisted to achieve more optimally in the human relations dimension. Then too, good attitudes may be developed in assisting in emotional development within learners. The present system of mandated learning with No Child Left Behind (NCLB) has no room for and does not stress social and emotional achievement. Pupils memorizing much content for NCLB testing are not learning to think which should be the ultimate goal of education. Thinking through what has been learned takes time and pupils need to possess the mental tools to think and make decisions, based on the best ideas available. Critical and creative thinking are definitely needed by pupils presently as well as in the future. The Masters Degree programme will offer the best for classroom teachers in objectives for pupil attainment.

Fourth, many university schools of education believe that four years of undergraduate course work in teacher education is inadequate for preparing today's teachers. I taught at Truman State University (Kirksville, Missouri) for over thirty years and we did away with the four year Baccalaureate degree for teacher preparation and now require all new teachers to possess the Master of Arts in Education (MAE), a five year degree for preservice teachers. It takes time to include all of what prospective teachers need to do well in public school teaching.

Fifth, professors in schools of education do much studying in determining what should be included in teacher education programmes. Most have earned doctorates from universities and have studied in depth that which is recommended in the education of teachers. It is largely university professors of education who write in educational journals and who keep up with reading of the literature in education. Many of these ideas are tried out in mini-lessons in the university classroom as well as in student teaching.

Most teacher educators who are professors of education with earned doctorates supervise student teachers in public school classrooms and have conferences following an observational visit to clarify objectives of instruction used, learning opportunities provided, and appraisal procedures used. The writer has participated in teaching a part of a unit when Supervising Student (ST) and regular teachers. Having taught in the Middle East at Friends boys School (Ramallah, Jordan, now the West Bank) and been engaged in relief work, has an excellent set of slides of Palestine. He made numerous return trips top this area and presented the audio visual aids in the social studies unit on The Middle

East. The scenes shown were very interesting to pupils on the walled city of Jerusalem, Bethlehem, Hebron and Samaria, in particular. Pupils being taught raised many salient questions pertaining to the slides followed by an indepth related discussion. University supervisors of student teachers have much to contribute in unit teaching taught by the preservice and regular teachers, resulting in a team approach as well as the ST teaching individually. A plethora of new ideas are brought into teaching and learning situations. This certainly is an advantage in emphasizing curriculum innovations with an MAE degree in teaching. Similar experiences may be brought into the MA degree following a four year traditional undergraduate BSE degree. A master's degree student cannot acquire enough rich experiences in emphasizing teaching and learning situations. A teachers realize they must find materials of instruction and methods of teaching which fit individual pupils in the classroom when providing for each pupil.

Conlcusion

The MA/MAE degree has much to recommend itself to enhance the quality of teaching pupils in the school setting. Pre and inservice teachers must be well educated to provide for all pupils in the school setting.

Merit Pay and Teacher

In many journal articles and teacher education conventions, the issue of merit pay is discussed and elaborated upon. Generally, teacher compensation is then tied to pupil achievement in test scores. Those who advocate this approach believe in the present system being outdated in determining teacher salaries which is based on level of university degrees obtained as well as years of teaching experience. The writer well recalls when he started teaching in the public schools in the early 1950s, a single salary schedule did not exist in most schools. The teacher who knew how to bargain with the administration/school board secured a higher salary than did other teachers in the same system. When more experienced teachers discovered that they did not receive as much salary as those who had less years of teaching experience and/or a lower level of university education, dissension set in and grievances occurred. There was then dissatisfaction within the teaching staff over how contracts were determined. This hindered the human relations element among teachers as well as the quality of teaching. Good teachers left the school system or the teaching profession when they felt being discriminated against. The single salary schedule resulted with salaries being based upon number of years taught within a school system and level of degrees secured such as the BSE and Master's degree.

Advocates of Merit Pay for Teachers

Advocates of merit pay state that teachers who perform better with pupil achievement should receive more salary than other teachers. A major problem seen here is, "How are we to determine better pupil performance in achievement?" Standardized tests are generally used in this measurement process. The writer has limited faith in standardized testing as a sole means of determining pupil achievement. When completing doctoral degree requirements, his university thesis committee was very cautious in the study to say that pupil achievement was higher in two categories with as compared to without having student teachers in pupil's classrooms. So my wording in the dissertation changed to state that "According to the Iowa Test of Basic Skills, pupils achieved significantly better with as compared to without university student teachers in the classroom. Why was the change advocated by my doctoral thesis committee? The results may have been different had the Metropolitan Achievement Test or the Stanford Achievement Test been used. The Iowa Test of Basic Skills is a reputable test and has high validity and reliability, measuring pupil skills achieved rather than subject matter content *per se*. There are additional reasons for limiting the use of standardized tests to ascertain learner progress in that they:

- tend to measure factual knowledge, not critical and creative thinking.
- limit in what is being measured, thus omitting the fine arts, (the social studies in the present No Child Left Behind law), health and physical education.

- do not ensure additional salient objectives be measured such as good human relations and being a caring person.
- are given once a year to make major decisions such as promoting/failing of pupils.

The writer is not against the use of standardized testing but would recommend its results be used to provide feedback for instruction. A printout of the standardized test results should clarify to the teacher what needs to be taught, reviewed, and emphasized. Properly written teacher developed tests as well as teacher observation may also be excellent methods to use in assessing pupil achievement.

In fact teacher observation may be the best means of appraisal since it might well be continuous with pupils receiving immediate assistance when needed. The criteria used here should reflect those which stress quality teaching and learning situations and emphasize high validity and reliability.

Comparisons Made by Critics

There are many news reports which criticize the American public schools, but give few/no suggestions in improvement. Seemingly, there is little understanding of what teaching is all about. Merit pay sounds easy to implement in that good teachers are rewarded with higher salary/bonuses and bad teachers are to be fired. Teachers in many cases are good or bad depending upon the environment they teach in. Thus, there may be thirty three pupils in a small classroom where the writer supervised a university student teacher. The aisles were too narrow to walk through. These pupils lacked motivation to achieve objectives, but they did entertain each other to keep others from achieving. Disrupting was easy since pupils could touch each other across the aisle, whisper, and wise crack to see who could top each other to secure laughs. In this case, the writer felt pupils were only learning negative things. In another school setting, there were thirteen mannerly pupils in the classroom in which reinforcement theory was utilized. Thus, the regular teacher and the student teacher could reward each step along the way in learning with a Santa Claus Stamp (It was the Christmas season), given on each page of every correct answer provided by each pupil on a work book page. This was possible with two teachers and thirteen pupils. It would be grossly unfair to have pupils achieve more optimally, when the playing field is not level in terms of pupil quality and number in learning. Other professions have much say so in terms of who to accept/reject as clientele. In the public schools, every child must be accepted and taught including future felons and the lawless.

Second, there are tremendously high costs involved in developing valid and reliable tests for the proposed Common Core Standards which then might be used to determine merit pay. The amount of money used to develop these standardized tests might be utilized more proficiently for other expenses in operating school systems. School systems have been laying off teachers and other school worker due to being in a recession. Class size needs to be kept low in number so that the teacher can give individual attention to learner needs in the classroom. Tests measure pupil achievement, not teacher quality of instruction. Thus, tests need to be designed to measure teaching quality in order to be valid and they must measure consistently to ascertain reliability. Unless the measurement instrument meets validity and reliability criteria, it is not appropriate to use in determining merit pay for teachers. Rewarding pupil test results with teacher pay incentives works in reverse to what teaching is all about and that is to optimize learner progress.

Third, it is difficult to measure what is truly important in any classroom. Selected behaviours are difficult to measure such as teacher dedication to the profession, being well prepared for each day of teaching, providing for individual differences among learners, and caring for each pupil to do as well as possible. If all teacher behaviours were to be listed for evaluation by school principals or through pupil appraisal, there would be an inordinate number of objectives to be appraised. For example, the teacher being able to make quality quick decisions in a problematic situation would be complex to determine as well as to measure numerically. Thus, there are many items to consider in teacher evaluation to determine merit pay as well as breaking down each to secure numerical results. Some decisions are more important than others and need to be made more rapidly within a given situation.

Fourth, morale problems may arise due to merit pay ratings given. Teachers individually might wonder why they did not secure the top rating. After all, the feeling could arise that much effort went into the delivery of education to pupils whereas it might appear that the ones receiving bonuses are not the teachers who put forth considerable effort into their teaching responsibilities. Generally, each teacher feels he/she should receive merit pay increases. Would the quality of teaching go downhill due to individual teachers feeling their efforts go unnoticed? After all, tests do not measure the highly specific qualities that go into teaching and learning endeavours. A few years ago, the administration and school board of a school system of 2000 students believed it would be good to reward the teacher of the month with a trophy. Upon voting on this procedure, teachers voted it down unanimously, feeling it would exacerbate morale problems. In this situation, teachers did not want this system of rewards. There would, indeed, be issues of fairness in giving the award. Objectivity would tend to be lacking in choosing the recipient.

Merit pay stresses the importance of offering money as rewards. Teachers tend not to go into teaching for monetary reasons. Service and humaneness are more salient factors. Good teachers are dedicated in assisting learners to achieve as well as possible in different facets of development, including good human relations. Thus, the physical, emotional, social, and moral development, as well as the academic are important. Since not all factors are measured in a valid and reliable way and might well be undocumented, the day to day workings of the teacher should also be assessed such as in utilizing observational methods in appraising the following characteristics:

- is the teacher well prepared for teaching, using either mandated procedures or a constructivism philosophy of instruction?
- is the teacher skillful in engaging all learners in the ongoing activity?
- do pupils feel the subject matter presented is relevant and purposeful?
- are a variety of methods used in teaching such as inductive/deductive methods, as well as problem solving?
- do pupils understand what is taught and presented in a meaningful endeavour?
- is the teacher enthusiastic in teaching and does the enthusiasm reflect within learners?

Each of the above asterisked items may be broken down into component parts such as "Is the teacher well prepared for teaching?" by perusing the daily lesson plan and observing its implementation. Thus, the following questions might arise in the process:

- are the objectives, learning activities, and evaluation procedures clearly stated?
- is the teacher skillful in implementing each part of the curriculum in the lesson plan?
- do pupils show evidence of achievement in reaching the objective(s)?
- were learners interested in the ongoing learning activities?
- do the evaluation procedures indicate validity and reliability?

- did pupils experience quality sequence in instructional delivery?

The classroom teacher is a prime mover of the school curriculum. However, the lay public, parents, and institutional groups also need to support optimally what teachers and pupils attempt to accomplish.

The writers have attempted to indicate the many variables involved in assisting pupils to achieve and there are a plethora involved. Merit pay is a difficult concept to devise and implement.

Emotional Intelligence and Teacher

The emotions possessed by a classroom teacher will, in part, determine human behaviour. Thus, the feelings possessed, be they positive or negative, do assist in ascertaining what will be emphasized or what will be done in the classroom setting. It behooves teachers to have training in controlling the emotions. The teacher with high a high Emotional Intelligence (El) will tend to have feelings of empathy toward others; understanding the feelings of others is salient. Too frequently, a teacher has said things which were regretted when reprimanding a pupil and then it takes time to heal the resultant wounds. Controlling personal feelings and knowing what irritates the self-needs reflection by the teacher.

Emotions and the Instructional Arena

Daniel Goleman (1995) is a leading advocate of Emotional Intelligence and how it affects relationships of teachers with others. EI stresses the need to emphasize the feeling dimension when expressing ideas. Thus, the individual has selected feelings toward a point of view, happening, or school of thought. It also assists in promoting achievement in regulating emotions to promote academic and emotional growth. Assessing one's own emotions is salient in that the following feelings hinder communication among school personnel:

- talking down to a person and/or using put downs.
- feelings of aloofness and superiority.
- rudeness and haughtiness in communicating with others.
- interrupting when others are speaking (Ediger and Rao, 2007).

It is important to be aware of the emotional dimension in each of the above named situations. When reflecting upon what transpired, the teacher might then think upon how these affected others as well as the self. Growth may then occur in modifying emotional achievement and development. Emotional control enters into the equation through diagnosis and remediation. New, innovative means of communication may come about whereby feelings of empathy result which stress acceptance and caring for others. Self-awareness means that one is understands personal feelings and how these might affect others (See Balaji, 2010).

A second dimension pertains to regulating one's feelings. Self-regulation brings in the management dimension of one's own feelings. By reflection, the communicator notices and thinks about what has transpired and the affect it has upon others. There are then points of importance in regulating the self pertaining to what might be offensive. The conscientious person regulates his/her feelings and adapts them to new situations. This minimizes guilt feelings in evaluating what has been said in oral communication. Teachers, too frequently, say things which are regretted later on such as saying to pupils:

- you always do sloppy school work!

- will you ever finish your assignments!
- don't be stupid, wake up!
- you won't amount to anything!

For each of the above asterisked items, the teacher may modify what was said to be more effective with sequential statements/comments including:

- lets work together so that you do neat work. I will show you how and then you may go ahead to work on neatness.
- be sure to complete each assignment. I will ask you periodically where you are specifically in completing an assignment.
- I will stand by your desk for a while to see if you have any problems so that you may keep working.
- Good work! Now go on to the next problem.

The teacher must try different ways to assist pupils in developing good habits in school and in society. The tone of voice and the choice of words utilized must come through in a respecting and caring for the child. Minimizing the child and his/ her feelings makes for dislike of the school and what it stands for. El emphasizes that pupils learn to like each curriculum area and that supports are available to assist in learning.

Motivation to learn comes from within the pupil in desiring to achieve. There is then commitment, drive, and initiative with success in learning being in evidence. The teacher may set the stage to motivate pupils by using a variety of interesting activities; thus, projects, reading experiences, problem solving, service activities, writing and speaking experiences, among others, assist pupils in staying the course. The teacher must observe signs from learners in terms of boredom, disinterest, and being distracted with the objective being to develop learner initiative (See Nazareth, 2010).

El stresses the importance of pupils developing social skills. Showing empathy is important in getting along well with others. This does not emphasize conformity behaviour, but rather creativity within the framework of achieving social skills. Problems must be identified and solutions sought in the human relations field. The tone of voice, stress of words, and pitch in oral communication convey feelings and intent of the communicator. Creativity is inherent when engaging in problem solving; innovative answers to new as well as old problems need possible solutions. The feeling dimension is involved in expressing thoughts, ideas and answers to problematic situations.

There are additional skills for teachers and pupils to develop which include:

- a spirit of optimism when encountering difficulties and related information must be sought in answer to these problems.
- intrinsically, feelings of success need to abound in school and in daily life.
- a belief in the self that one is capable of living harmoniously with others.
- being a responsible individual for personal happiness and positive feelings of emotion.
- an ability to cope with life and life's problems.
- showing respect for the feelings of others.
- being honest with the self and with others.
- being receptive to non-verbal communication (See Varney, 2010).

Testing, Measurement and Behaviourism

Behaviourism is a somewhat opposite approach in educational philosophy. It stresses teachers/educators determining objectives prior to instruction. These are considered vital objectives in teaching/learning, are stated in measurable terms and are highly specific, leaving little/

no leeway for interpretation. Teachers then teach toward having pupils achieve the objectives. Generally, leading educational companies are presently chosen to write mandated objectives and accompanying standardized tests. The tests must have high validity and reliability, be standardized, which permit pupils' results being compared against the standardization group. Standardized test results allow for making comparisons—one pupil against another. Thus a pupil's test results may indicate he/she is on the fortieth percentile meaning out of every 100 pupils taking the test, 60 are above and forty below. Or, a pupil being on the 10th percentile indicates that out of every 100 pupils taking the test, 90 are above and 10 below that level. Norms were developed from a random sampling of pupils taking the pilot studies for the test which ultimately was standardized. Any score obtained by the teacher's pupils might then be compared with scores of the standardization group, listed in the accompanying Manual (Ediger and Rao, 2003).

Standardized tests are, in part, due to indicating how validity and reliability were obtained, who was in the pilot study to represent a random sampling, how the norms were developed, and what is meant by standardization. With standardization, the following uniform criteria must be adhered to:

- the directions are the same for all test takers.
- the time limits are the same for all involved in test taking.
- no hints are given to any one during the time the test is taken.
- the key for computer scoring is the same for each age level of test takers.

The only variable from the above asterisked items is the pupil taking the test which includes inherent motivation, interest, past experiences, and perceived purposes. Thus, the debate continues with behaviourists believing that:

- objectives for pupil achievement need to stated prior to teaching a lesson/unit of study.

- knowledge, skills, and attitudinal objectives achieved by pupils are measurable and need to be stated precisely so there is, preferably, no leeway for interpretation.
- generally, multiple choice test items are used to measure pupil achievement. Thus, only one of the distractors represent a correct answer.
- with computerized scoring, mass number of tests are scored within a state in a short time.

REFERENCES

Balaji, P. S. (2010), *Impact of Locus of Control in Emotional Intelligence*, Academic Self Image and Self Assessment of Students of Colleges of Education in Chennai. Ph. D. Thesis evaluated by the writer (Ediger) for Alagappa University, Karaikudi, India.

Ediger, Marlow, and D. Bhaskara Rao (2007), *Teaching Social Studies*. New Delhi, India: Discovery Publishing House.

Ediger, Marlow, and D. Bhaskara Rao (2003), *Philosophy and Curriculum*. New Delhi, India; Discovery Publishing House.

Goleman, Daniel (1995), *Emotional Intelligence*. New York; Bantam Books.

Nazareth, Bruno D. (2010), *Effect of Emotional Intelligence and Self Efficacy* of B. Ed. Trainees on their Academic Achievement. Ph. D. Thesis evaluated by the writer for Alagappa University, India.

Varney, James J. (2010), *"The Role of Dissertation Self Efficacy in Increasing Dissertation Completion;* Sources, Effects and Visibility of a New Self Efficacy Construct," College Student Journal, 44 (4) 932-947.

CHAPTER 27

Teacher Tenure and Union Membership

Tenure for teachers strengthens the teaching profession in a plethora of ways. It takes selected uncertainties out of life. Pupils tend to receive a better education because teachers feel more secure and do not have to worry continuously if they will be able to return to work without having the threats of, "You are fired." There needs to be a certain amount of stability in knowing that one is employed for a certain period of time if satisfactory teaching occurs. Tenure is given to a teacher upon four to five years of satisfactory teaching experience. Later, if a teacher has received unsatisfactory ratings by a supervisor, and this is documented over a period of time, he/she may be dismissed or it may be challenged legally. Legal representation is available by either the National Education Association (NEA) or the American Federation of Teachers (AFT), depending on who holds the current membership for the teacher. The teacher may also choose to resign upon hearing the negative news of incompetency. The purpose for tenure is to protect good teachers from arbitrary dismissal, not to protect the bad teacher. A powerful person in a community having a grudge against a teacher can work havoc. Then too, tenure assists in guarding against unreasonable demands upon teachers. Too many pupils or too many unruly children in a classroom may bring in a union consultant who represents the teacher. An excellent teacher who had ten years of teaching experience was given a very unruly pupil; she almost resigned at Christmas time. Unions are there to assist in working out problematic situations. There are two dimensions in employment—the organization and the teacher, each having their rights.

Quality Teaching and Tenure

After receiving tenure, the teacher must definitely not become complacent. Tenure is there to protect against arbitrary dismissal of teachers. Good teachers must be protected so they may continues to do well in educating children and not fear instability in the professional arena. They too, however, worry about unprofessional decisions made. Teachers deemed to be incompetent or indifferent need assistance to improve teaching and learning situations. Opportunities are there to improve on those listed deficiencies in time. Dismissal can be a likely situation, and there are weak performers in any profession.

Good teaching emphasizes definite criteria and there must be acceptable procedures in realizing these goals. Thus, for example, inservice education might occur at faculty meetings. Here, a rotating committee needs to develop an agenda with suggestions from faculty members in terms of what is to be covered pertaining to curriculum improvement. These items must be clearly spelled out and in the hands of participants two days prior to the faculty meeting. Faculty meetings preclude much planning by the teacher to meet goals of agenda items. Thus, reading recent educational journals to be highly knowledgeable pertaining grouping pupils for instructional purposes is a readiness activity. Out of the faculty meeting, committees may be formed pertaining to each item deemed highly salient on the agenda. Each committee has a deadline to meet in reporting their findings to the total faculty. Indepth studies need to be made and the results might be implemented in whole or in part. Sharing of ideas in their implementation provide ideas for curriculum improvement to others.

A second inservice education idea to emphasize is a workshop concept. Here, faculty members are surveyed on what needs to be studied in order to advance curriculum improvement. A consensus might result in which faculty members agree upon studying, for instance, how to increase learner involvement in the curriculum. A thorough discussion based on related research, talking with other professionals, and results from implementation of innovative ideas may spike enthusiasm for the workshop. Each teacher needs to participate freely and openly in discussions relating to definite conclusions. The success of the workshop depends upon the enthusiasm and motivation of participants in desiring to improve the curriculum.

A third form of inservice education is to take courses at an approved university. The end result must be on strengthening one's subject matter and skills in teaching. A course on the psychology of learning needs to stress content and an internship on quality teaching and learning. Topics such as intrinsic/extrinisc motivation, the affective dimension in learning, meeting needs of learners, grouping for instruction, as well as diversity in assessment of learner progress are must! Ideas acquired from taking university courses should be tried out in the teacher's classroom and shared in the class setting.

A fourth means of inservice education is for the teacher to do an approved individual study. The study should be intensive and emphasize relevant, useful information on a specific area of teaching such as discipline in the classroom setting. Here, the teacher may secure content on assertive discipline, reinforcement theory, zero tolerance, among others. Facets of these contributions may be tried out in the classroom and discussed with other teachers. Meaning must be attached to each plan of discipline. The strengths and weaknesses of discipline procedures provide food for contemplation. Modifications may be made in order to be useful in the local classroom.

Opportunities need to be available for teachers to attend state and national conferences in diverse academic disciplines with the intent of curriculum improvement. Curriculum improvement stresses the importance of quality teaching which should assist in the area of using approved disciplinary procedures. Classroom management procedures has as a starting point the providing of situations conducive to learning.

By following vital schools of thought in acceptable procedures of disciple and of curriculum improvement, the teacher strengthens his/her position in receiving and maintaining tenure. There are times, however, when a supervisor may desire to get rid of a teacher due to factors not involving quality teaching and/or good human relationships with learners. Silent harassment of individual teachers is practiced until a satisfactory teacher might become very frustrated and might even resign. Thus, for example, the supervisor may

- come into the classroom and seated in the back of the classroom, write supposedly endless observational notes. This may occur frequently whereas previously this was not done.
- not greet or speak to the classroom teacher, but put notices in his/her mailbox even though this could have been communicated in a face to face situation. This happened also to a university colleague of mine whereby the Head of the Division did not communicate orally

with the professor, but stuck notices, major or minor, on the office door even though the professor was in his office. The professor, being deeply hurt, could not accept this behaviour and resigned at the end of the school year. Shunning is definitely a form of harassment.

- give unsatisfactory ratings to a teacher who received high commendations from other teachers, parents and children.
- assign an unsatisfactory classroom to a teacher. For instance, a teacher in the writer's university summer graduate class told of having severe arthritis in the knees, but was given a classroom on the third floor of the building which had no elevator.
- provide the elementary teacher with a classroom next to a drinking fountain. When the bell rang for a change of classes, middle school pupils, standing in line for a drink of water, would rap on the elementary classroom door. This happened several times a day and did much disrupting of pupil behaviour. This was repeatedly reported to the school principal who failed to act in changing the situation.

A union representative can be called in with attempts made to remedy the situation. There needs to be harmonious relationships among employees for a school to function well. Good attitudes is essential for teachers to do well in school. Otherwise, there may be much worrying about being able to endure until the end rather that to focus on good teaching. The teacher alone may not be able to solve some of the above named problems by the self but collectively with a union can change many things from the negative to the positive. Tenure is a way to develop feelings of confidence and security in developing and working toward improved instruction. Thought must be placed upon assisting pupils to achieve optimally rather than worrying about retention of that teacher.

Conclusion

There are two dimensions in teaching and learning situations with the classroom teacher representing one point on the continuum with the institution representing the other end. Both are salient with the individual producing a service which is teaching and education of pupils, the other being the institution—the public schools. The teacher as an individual is employed by a grant represented by the school system. The teacher has rights which may receive protection by the union. By the self, the teacher has little influence but collectively with union assistance can provide for a more level playing field with that of the institution, the public schools. Collectively, both may work together to improve the curriculum for all pupils. Involved problems need to be ignored out.

Self-efficacy and School Administrator

Self-efficacy is a valuable concept for school administrators to possess. To become efficacious, a knowledgeable principal continues to grow, develop, and achieve in the school setting. A wide variety of means need to be used for continuous inservice education; self-efficacy is a goal to pursue in time and place. Self-efficacy brings on self-confidence and an inward desire to do well in educational and life's endeavours. These feelings are necessary in order to do the best possible in the profession of teaching and learning. Each pupil in the 21st century must attain as much as possible in this technological and computer based environment.

Becoming Efficacious in School Administration

Self-efficacy involves believing in one self to do well in daily and complex situations demanded in school administration. Trusting in the self to make quality decisions is quite different from doubt and mistrust in facing situations involving decision-making choices in the school setting. Cognitively, the principal believes he/she has necessary concepts and generalizations, as well as skills, to size up curricular choices which must be made. Beliefs are there to sustain qualities needed for selecting and choosing from among alternatives. Within the school setting, the school administrator works in a social environment. Thus, clarity in communicating ideas is necessary which brings linguistic theory into situations involving speaking and writing to convey content necessary to fulfil obligations in developing/managing teaching and learning. Meaningful communication stresses the need for proper stress, pitch, and juncture in oral communication while in written communication, this can be shown with ending punctuation marks such as exclamatory, interrogative, declarative/imperative sentences (Ediger and Rao, 2003).

Body language such as facial expressions, gestures, and physical movement convey messages to the listener. Self awareness of personal feelings in these situations can make for better human relations and skills. People behaviour is necessary in thinking about getting along harmoniously with others. This does not mean conformity in mannerisms; creativity is always significant in that uniqueness is present in tackling difficult issues. Tradition might not work in solving problems due to each problem being different from others. New ideas must be brought into harmonize with solving pupil problems in learning (Ediger, 2010).

Self-efficacy may be increased with study, research, learning from others, and through human interaction. The following then become salient for the school administrator:

- reading recent journal articles on Emotional Intelligence (El) pertaining to administration, supervision, and curriculum.
- attend professional state/national meetings including the National Association for Secondary School Principals, and the National Association of Elementary School Principals (USA), among others, and attend sessions on EI.

- have a qualified person speak on El to teachers, with opportunities of interaction with the speaker.
- do a research study on emotional Intelligence (See Goleman, 1998).

Successful experiences in school and in society assist in building confidence in one's own thoughts and actions. The school administrator needs to work with his/her staff in helping pupils succeed in the different curriculum areas in school. Good social relations must be established and needs emphasis over time. Self-efficacy stresses the importance of a knowledgeable, well adjusted person. This person beliefs in the worth of his/her ideas and also has the ability to listen carefully to others in an atmosphere of respect and acceptance.

In addition to success in life, self-efficacy also emphasizes vicarious experiences learning from models to emulate. Confident well adjusted persons might well provide acceptable models. Thus, there are highly motivated people who exhibit desirable achievements; these individuals may have persevered through difficulties. "We learn from the behaviours of others in society," who have done well in life. Vicarious learning is salient since an individual might not have the same experiences as the one being emulated, but can learn to adapt as well as be creative. Vicarious experiences then provide role models for individuals to emulate. Then too, individuals may be encouraged to do more challenging task than what was originally believed. Many individuals have reached out to become something greater than originally intended due to direct and vicarious experiences (See Bandura, 1997).

The writer was persuaded by a professor at a university he was enrolled in that securing the doctorate in education would be an excellent pathway to follow, following completion of the MA degree. The encouragement, from among other professors and sources, never left my thinking of a future profession. Encouragement is important for a person to go onto a higher status or position in education. Minimizing a person to feel inferior might be illustrated by a degrading comment the writer faced was the following in a high school English class:

> My short story titled, "Murder on the Second Floor," was voted by classmates to be the best product in the class of 25 students. I mentioned to the instructor that I was surprised in receiving the award. Having grown up as a Mennonite, humility was prized highly. The instructor looked down upon me and stated that my paper was very poorly written and she wondered why students had voted the way they did."

Teachers need to be careful in being positive when assisting learners to develop a good self-concept. Comments made by teachers and principals who are role models are taken seriously. School principals need to work with staff members in assisting pupils to become self-efficacious when commenting on the latter's progress. Pupils' successes build upon each other of what was experienced previously. Social persuasion is a valuable approach in assisting pupils to improve their lot in life. Principals of schools have numerous opportunities to guide learner success in life. By taking note of pupil achievement in school and awards received outside of school, the principal can assist learners individually toward success in life. Being interested in pupils makes it possible to make major contributions toward a learner moving forward in life. Commenting personally to a high school student about possibilities in a future career/profession based on achievement/leadership in the curriculum or student activities may become a turning point in a positive direction for the involved student in achievement. The following areas of student accomplishments provide ground work for these comments:

- grade point average and/or consistently high progress made on projects in classes taken.

- notable achievements and progress made in Boy and Girl Scouts, 4H, FFA, among other activities.
- concern shown toward others as well as assistance given in particular situations.
- perseverance and motivation revealed in pursuing a specific objective.

Self appraisal is important when facing stressful situations. The attempt should be made to look within the self then, when stress reduction is being emphasized. The school principal must face life as it truly is with the intention of minimizing that which comes in the way of achievement, such as excess anxiety and tension. Stress reduction may come about when office work does not accumulate, but is handled as quickly as possible. Discipline problems come and go, but must be dealt with a humane and responsible way. Breathing deeply and thinking positively aids in minimizing stress in these cases. Making proper referrals when increased professional help is needed in dealing with discipline problems provides situations in which the principal feels he/she is not alone in difficult situations. Each school/school district has a hand book outlining procedures to take in taking care of discipline. This provides comfort to the school administrator in minimizing stress when referring to problems involving discipline. Each case must be handled with respect and empathy; pupil self-concepts continue to evolve. By building and developing procedures to follow in the disciplinary arena, the school principal becomes more self-confident and efficacious in dealing with the unknown. By reflecting upon what was done, the principal may diagnose and remediate with the result being improved methods and techniques to utilize. He/she is always a rote model to emulate. If the principal has patience, is conscientious, and has learner interests at heart, pupils will feel that quality leadership is there to make school achievement possible (See Goleman, 1995).

REFERENCES

Bandura, Albert (1997), *Self-Efficacy, The Exercise of Control.* New York: Freeman.

Ediger, Marlow (2010), Portfolios in the Social Studies, College Student Journal, 44 (4), 913-915.

Ediger, Marlow, and D. Bhaskara Rao (2003), *Language Arts Curriculum.* New Delhi, India: Discovery Publishing House.

Goleman, Daniel (1998), *Working With Emotional Intelligence.* New York: Bantam Books.

Goleman, Daniel (1995), *Emotional Intelligence.* New York: Bantam Books.

CHAPTER 29

Supervision of Instruction in School Settings

There are a plethora of variables which affect teaching and learning situations. The supervisor needs to evaluate what helps and what hinders the instructional process. An analysis of variables and factors then need to be viewed in order to deliver the best learning opportunities possible under the circumstances with a goal of helping the teacher use what exists and acquire that which might well benefit the teaching and learning process. The role of the supervisor is to help teachers to deliver the best instruction possible. This is difficult in selected situations with large class size, inadequate instructional materials, and challenging pupils in the classroom, among others. The teacher, however, needs to do the best possible in reaching each pupil in the classroom to optimize instruction.

The Role of the Supervisor

Each supervisor must have a vision of what to accomplish which needs to be shared with participants. The vision provides a framework for improving instruction. These goals then provide a plan or structure for curriculum improvement. There are selected knowledge, skills, and attitudes which need to be developed by pupils. The supervisor plans with teachers on how to bring innovative ideas to the forefront. He/she brings to the school setting a concept of wholeness. Thus, the supervisor has feelings, values, and attitudes toward the self, others, and the curriculum. He/she also possesses selected skills in working with others. Hopefully, quality human relations will be revealed along with caring, knowledgeable, and helpful dispositions to encourage human interaction. Put downs, rudeness, and talking down to others will be minimized or eliminated. Communication with teachers must be positive to bring important curriculum considerations to the forefront. Ideas, beliefs, and diverse philosophies of instruction need to be analyzed and discussed. The best of these need to be honed and, implemented on an experimental basis.

One role of the supervisor should be that of studying quality research studies in order to bring these to the attention of teachers. An atmosphere of respect must be in evidence in the communication process, not one of haughtiness. In my experiences as university supervisor of student teachers, the following complaints were presented of those in their respective schools of supervisory experiences:

- dogmatic ideas in believing there is only one right way of proceeding
- ridiculing suggestions which were not on the supervisor's agenda
- aloofness with negative feelings toward teachers
- hostility in general.

Fortunately, there are a minimal number of supervisors fitting the above categories. Supervision involves interacting with teachers and support staff in a positive manner; there is much work that needs to be done in any situation and schools are no exception with curriculum improvement endeavours. There are numerous points of intervention for supervisors in assisting teachers to improve teaching and learning situations. One point might well be to assist the teacher in getting all pupils involved in learning. Too Frequently, some pupils get left out of being the involvement process. When supervising university student teachers, the writer found this to be a problem in the classroom. A conscientious effort needs to be in the offing for teachers to provide adequately for *each* learner. It is something which necessitates effort and reflection to ascertain that which can be done to secure the interests of each pupil. Metacognition skills then must be honed to secure the interests of pupils be it thorough a change of learning opportunities, of peer interaction, or difficulty level of learning activities provided.

As a possible second point of intervention, meaning must be established by pupils. Pupils then might not have understood what was explained to the class as a whole and selected individuals need more assistance. Thus, a pupil may need help in word recognition skills as in using context clues. Sometimes, pupils make wild guesses at unknown words and these do not fit into the contextual situation. Guiding learners to make sense of subject matter read with the use of context clues is a valuable skill that transfers to many situations. The supervisor may need to model this procedure clearly to the teacher involved in assisting the learner. Demonstrating how to perform a teaching suggestion is a necessary responsibility of the supervisor of instruction.

Third, pupils may meet higher expectations, as compared to where he/she is now presently attaining, through the use of scaffolding. Pupils might be assisted to achieve more optimally, but need help to do so within a specific learning situation. A quality supervisor may be better able to evaluate this as compared to a classroom teacher who is near to the scene. Thus, the supervisor suggests possibilities in scaffolding achievement. This does not mean forcing higher achievement, but it does indicate the possibilities of sequencing activities to realize the higher level. Teachers need to be aware that subject matter being learned needs to make sense, be understandable, as well as meaningful. Merely memorizing content does not assist the pupil to realize higher levels of cognition, since ensuing experiences are based on the previous leanings acquired and to harmonize the two sequentially must be a seamless as possible.

Fourth, the supervisor may see a need to work with a small group of teachers when a new procedure is to be emphasized. Thus, for instance, when response through intervention (RTI) is being brought into an elementary school, the supervisor meets with these teachers to introduce RTI. The goals and purposes, the testing procedures for intervention, and assessment providing information to the teacher in proceeding with ensuing learning experiences must be experienced by teachers when working with a set of pupils in reading instruction. Clarity of communication is of utmost importance so that teachers understand the underlying ideas of RTI and methods of implementing the programme. Supervision of instruction is very important here in that careful implementation of the innovation proceeds. Individual and small group supervision is salient in improving the curriculum.

Fifth, the teaching faculty of a school may also be involved in quality supervision. Thus, there are times to meet with the entire faculty when, for example, demonstration teaching is stressed. Committee endeavours may not have been stressed or was unfavourably implemented in the classroom setting by teachers. The supervisor needs to clarity the implementation of successful collaborative work in the classroom. A group of four to five pupils may be used in the demonstration teaching plan. Thus, the supervisor introduces, briefly, background knowledge necessary for small group work. Thus, a concrete or semi-concrete experience such as video tape or DVD content may provide the necessary readiness activity. This is followed by a discussion of the audio-visual video involving the four/five pupils in the demonstration teaching experience. Pointers to emphasize in working with committees in the classroom setting include the following:

- each needs to participate but no one dominate the discussion.
- members of the committee must stay on the topic.
- problems and questions should arise during the discussion.
- the responses may be pursued during the allotted time and extended to a later project/activity.
- clarity in communicating ideas is salient.

Sixth, developing a professional library with/for teachers, support personnel and school administrators containing educational journals, relevant textbooks in teacher education, as well as other materials of inservice education should be an inherent part of the regular school library. The contents of the professional library need to be publicized among professionals in the school setting. Hopefully, the professional library will have participants do considerable reading and viewing AV aids from these sources which might well provide information for discussion at faculty meetings. Major ideas may then be considered for curriculum improvement. Feedback from implementation should be shared with faculty members. Content needs to circulate among faculty/staff with worthwhile ideas being shared in the school culture.

Seventh, teachers should have ample opportunities to observe other teachers teach and discuss observations made with the involved teacher. There should be opportunities for teacher interaction so that learning from other professionals may be stressed. There needs to be ample opportunities to discuss objectives, learning activities, and evaluation procedures used in teaching and learning situations. Analyzing and synthesizing of ideas discussed should be mentally stimulating to improve the curriculum. Professionals have an inward desire to improve instruction in order to provide for individual differences.

Conclusion

Supervisory leadership must encourage teachers to move from what is to what should be in a normative way. It is difficult to provide for individual differences in any classroom, but continual striving to do so is the role of the professional teacher. Individual differences in academic achievement, social and physical development among learners may be great indeed in any classroom, and the teacher has responsibilities in meeting needs to assist learners to accomplish well in an increasingly complex world.

Managing the Classroom

A very salient responsibility in teaching and learning situations is Classroom Management. A knowledgeable teacher may fail in teaching due to inability to work effectively with pupils. Thus, pupils may be entertaining each other during class time, talking aloud incessantly, walking around aimlessly in the classroom, and bother others, among other annoyances.

But, what can be done to help pupils team in these situations?

- very careful planning of each lesson so that pupils realize the seriousness of teaching and learning.
- keep the lesson moving forward to minimize interruptions.
- engage pupils with interesting activities.
- observe pupils continuously to keep them on task.
- stand next to the initial disrupter while teaching.
- give honest praise to pupils doing good work.

- knowledgeable resource persons must be available when solving misbehaviours problems and work out a plan for improving classroom discipline. The school district must also have a discipline manual for teachers to follow (Ediger and Rao, 2007).

The above asterisked items provide direction and guidance for improving teaching and learning situations.

Grouping pupils for instruction needs to be planned very carefully. There are times when pupils achieve best in a homogeneously grouped situation, such as in teaching reading to a group of talented elementary school aged learners. These pupils may challenge each other in positive ways, especially in discussion situations whereby higher levels of cognition involving critical and creative thinking as well as problem solving are involved. Needs of learners, also, to determine which pupils go into a group such as when diagnoses in remedial reading is stressed as in a small group of pupils needing assistance in utilizing context clues to identify unknown words (See Vygotsky, 1933-1978).

The class as a whole provides opportunities for pupils to be introduced to a new unit of study in the social studies whereby all might view an audio-visual presentation. The teacher may point out specifics within the activity to enhance achievement. At the beginning, during, and at the end of the AV presentation, he/she may lead pupils in discussing answers to questions. Problem areas might be identified and committees formed to research relevant items (Kumar and Hablemariam (2010).

In science, the class as a whole might observe a demonstration or experiment. The activity must possess clarity for all to observe what is transpiring. Adequate background information must be presented so the pupils will attach meaning to the ensuing-experiences. Small groups might be established with members interacting to clarify ideas. Mannerly movement to form each group needs emphasis (See Nieto, *et.al.,* 2010-2011).

A mathematics teacher, for example, teaching the class as a whole, might show with the use of manipulative materials regrouping of numbers necessary in division. Learners must understand in a meaningful manner what transpires when renaming occurs. Pupils need to attach meaning sequentially to concepts presented. Previous leanings are needed to acquire new subject matter ideas with pupils perceiving the relationship of ideas (Tucker, *et.al.* (2010).

Pupil progress is observed when the mathematics teacher observes learners working on the assigned activities. Diagnosis and remediation is involved with pupils individually being guided in correcting errors, either inductively or deductively. Peer mediated instruction may also be used if there is a knowledgeable person, providing leadership, in each small group.

Peer interaction is a preferred learning style of selected learners. This needs to be emphasized in the classroom along with other styles such as:

- explanations/short lectures presented by the teacher. The content with the use of purposeful instructional aids must be well planned, clearly presented with prosody. Homogeneous or heterogeneous groups may then be formed to enrich and extend understandings.
- project methods whereby committee members have a purpose in developing a project directly related to the ongoing unit of study. The purpose emphasizes planning and clarifying an abstract concept into the semi-concrete and concrete such as making a model, dramatizing a written play, co-operatively developing notebooks which cover content within a unit of study, among others. Carrying out the plans and evaluating the final product are also parts of the activity.
- debates involving a societal issue, following the rules for debating involved learners as well as being on their

developmental level. Adequate research must be done to support the side of the debating team. The research materials used involve the computer, basal textbooks, and encyclopedias, among others (See Baildon and Baildon, 2008).

For each of the above asterisked items, the teacher must use proper management procedures to optimize learning and minimize disruptions. Good classroom managers are well prepared and possess foresight to avoid pupil misbehaviour. Thus, in grouping for instruction, pupils need to move their chairs quietly and orderly from one group to the next method of arranging pupils for instruction. Much noise and disorder may transpire if a smooth arrangement is not in evidence. It is more difficult then for learners to be attentive and concentrate on the tasks at hand. Pupils can be taught to pick up their chairs quietly and quickly to move on to an ensuing experience involving a seating arrangement. Learning proper manners is important in the classroom setting (See Moeller, 2005). In discussions, for instance, pupils must experience quality guidelines which

- do not interrupt while a participant is speaking in a committee setting.
- listen carefully to each participant and ask for clarification if content expressed is not clear or questions arise.
- speak clearly and stay on the topic being discussed.
- ideas during the discussion need to circulate among committee members with no one dominating the free flow of ideas.

Discipline and the Curriculum

There may be cases where special procedures need emphasis to aid in classroom management. Each school board should possess a manual in the arena of discipline. Zero Tolerance has been adopted by a few. This is a strict procedure of discipline. Thus, for example, there may be a rule whereby possession of a knife in school makes for suspension for a designated period of time such as three days to a week. A news headlines few years ago mentioned a short finger nail file carried by an elementary pupil to school. This was considered to be a knife by the school administration. The boy had not been in previous trouble but was suspended. The interpretation can be very strict as to what the intended use was. There is a huge difference between an eight inch sharp hunting knife and a short finger nail file. And yet to define these specifics could amount to a large volume of disciplinary items. To be sure, bringing the hunting knife or a loaded pistol to school must have dire consequences. A few pupils may be expelled due to the danger involved to others. These, however, must receive home schooling provided by the local school district.

Less stringent than Zero Tolerance is assertive discipline whereby the teacher writes the pupil's name on the board for the first offense in agreed upon rules of conduct, posted on the bulletin board. After three offenses, the pupil is sent to the principal's office indicating what the pupil had done to warrant this. Upon return to the classroom, the teacher notices if the pupil's behaviour is conducive to learning. In my graduate class Theory of Administration, three students teaching in the same school complained about their high school principal being a very kind, likable and considerate person who in faculty meetings always invited his teachers to send to his office misbehaving pupils with discipline problems. The problem was, according to these three teachers, that pupils behaved the same or even worse when coming back to the classroom.

With practice, the teacher may find ways that work in curbing discipline problems. He/she needs to use all of the suggestions on teaching and learning in this manuscript to see what works generally and in specific situations. This should include searching the literature, using internet and other reference sources; in securing ideas to implement in humane approaches that which is conducive to solve problems relating to discipline and classroom management. There are a plethora of sources available for assistance. It is important to discuss with other professionals as to what helps in the area of disciplinary problems. The teacher should never give up in providing a classroom which helps pupils to achieve objectives of instruction in cognition, in skills, and in attitudinal dimensions.

REFERENCES

Baildon, Rindi, and Mark Baildon (2008), *"Guiding Independence: Developing a Research Tool to Support Student Decision Making in Selecting Outline Information Sources,"* The Reading Teacher, 61(8), 636-658.

Ediger, Marlow, and D. Bhaskara Rao (2007), *Teaching Social Studies.* New Delhi, India: Discovery Publishing House, Chapters One and Two.

Kumar, Saheesh, and Rezene Hablemariam (2010), *"Learning with Multimedia; A Constructive Co-operative Approach in Education,"* Edutrends, 15-18.

Moeller, K. (2005), *"Creating Zones of Possibilities for Struggling Readers,"* Journal of Literacy Research, 36 (4), 419-450.

Nieto, Sonia, *et. al.* (2010-2011), *"What Makes a Great Teacher?"* Educational Leadership, 68(4), 74-76.

Tucker, Carolyn, *et.al.,* (2010), *"Using Children's Literature to Teach Mathematics,"* Reading Improvement, 47 (3), 154-161.

Vygotsky, Len (1933-1978), *Mind in Society: The Development of Higher Psychological Processes.* Cambridge, Massachusetts: Harvard University Press.

Index